Anglo-Catholic
Church Planting

Can it work?

— JOHN WALLACE —

Sacristy
Press

Sacristy Press
PO Box 612, Durham, DH1 9HT

www.sacristy.co.uk

First published in 2023 by Sacristy Press, Durham

Sacristy Limited, registered in England & Wales, number 7565667

British Library Cataloguing-in-Publication Data
A catalogue record for the book is available from the British Library

ISBN 978-1-78959-297-9

Contents

Preface

This book is based on my doctoral thesis on Anglo-Catholic church planting. It arose from the experience of the church which I attend and where I had been churchwarden (twice) previously, and a member of the Parochial Church Council for many years.[1] It is a liberal Catholic church in what was a small market town but is now much more of a commuter town with a number of large new housing developments. The parish is part of a Team Benefice with a growing population at the time of writing of around 47,000, the largest benefice in the diocese, and my constituent parish itself is one of the largest parishes in the diocese with over 28,000 parishioners.

Some 14 years ago (at the time of writing), there was concern about the lack of active Christian witness on the new large Southern Housing development in our parish. Prior to this, the parish had contributed significant funding to share with the diocese to buy a house to be designated as a vicarage to demonstrate at least a Christian presence in this new housing area. However, although providing a visible Christian presence with a house named as St Michael's Vicarage, neither the priest who first moved into this house nor his successor as Team Vicar had the time or freedom to engage in what in reality was a pioneer situation, as they had other responsibilities within the Team Ministry. This is not in any way a criticism of their ministries but rather a gradual realization that something different was needed and that God gives different gifts to people in the church (cf. 1 Corinthians 12). This growing concern then coincided with a vacancy, as the Team Vicar living in that vicarage moved on to another post.

---

[1] The Parochial Church Council—the elected decision-making body in a Church of England parish.

After considerable discussion within both the parish and the wider team, especially in respect of the financial and workload implications, it was agreed to appoint a Pioneer Priest, instead of a traditional Team Vicar, to live in the vicarage and to work in those estates. Those of us involved were not really sure about what to expect of such a person, nor indeed what he/she would do, beyond being the more visible focus of a Christian presence and activity.

An appointment was made of an ordained and experienced Church Army captain, very much supported by his wife, and he was given a "blank canvas". He said that in seven years, there would be an established worshipping congregation meeting on the estate. The first thing that he and his wife did was to make the ground floor of their three-storey vicarage available for a toddler group. They also made their presence known around the estate both by leafleting and by very visible daily dog-walking. They were soon asked by some people, who had vaguely heard about Messy Church, to start one in the Community House (a typical three-bedroomed semi-detached house loaned by the developers for a period of five years for some undefined "community purpose"). Over 40 people attended the first session, which far exceeded the safe capacity of the house and so they decided to run two sessions a month on a ticketed basis because the venue was so constricted in its capacity.

A new school had been planned some time ago for the area and when it belatedly opened, the governors and headteacher agreed that it could be used for worship on Sundays. The Pioneer Minister and his wife also agreed to be keyholders which reduced the hiring fees. This became the worship centre for what was soon designated as a Conventional District,[2] with regular weekly Anglican worship—not in an Anglo-Catholic format

---

[2] In the Church of England, a conventional district is a defined area placed under the care of a curate in charge (called the Minister of the Conventional District) with a district church council, by agreement between the incumbent(s) and bishop. They are not parishes but can have all the apparatus of a parish. They are often thought of as experimental parishes pending their creation as proper parishes in their own right. <https://www.churchofengland.org/sites/default/files/2017-10/mission_and_pastoral_measure_2011_-_volume_2.pdf>, accessed 18 January 2023.

but most definitely liturgically structured. Initially, a small number of people from the parish church attended to give support and provide some experience to what was probably a quite "dechurched" congregation, that is, those who had some previous, but not recent experience of church, both Anglican and other denominations. However, local leadership soon emerged, and the church was able to appoint two churchwardens and elect a church council. The parish church agreed to fund a portion of the stipend of the Pioneer Minister, on an annual and tapering basis from 2016 up to the end of 2020 as part of its commitment to mission. (The church has since moved from the school, which it has outgrown, and now meets in the Community Centre and, after worship, provides refreshments for the many football teams that play on the adjacent football pitches—a valued outreach ministry.)

Seeing what was happening and that significant missional activity was taking place, I asked myself why, if my church was doing this, other churches of the same tradition were not doing similar things in their parishes? I resolved to learn more about any Anglo-Catholic-based church plants that were in existence, especially as the report *From Anecdote to Evidence* supports the idea that church planting should take place in all parts of the Church of England. As regards Anglo-Catholic churches it says, "This model is still being developed and there is on-going reflection about what planting means in an Anglo-Catholic context."[3]

It was a challenge for me to undertake such research, but I also wanted to understand whether current church plants actually fitted into the way Anglo-Catholicism had developed in the nineteenth century and if some aspects of what had been done in that period in relation to the founding of new churches were applicable and transferable to support current church planting. I therefore approached the admissions tutor of the Durham University Doctorate of Theology and Ministry Programme with my ideas. I was accepted on the course for September 2015. I also wanted to include some form of historical comparison alongside my physical research. My aim was that my research would be a real piece of Practical

---

[3]   *From Anecdote to Evidence: Findings from the Church Growth Research Programme 2011–2013* (London: The Church Commissioners for England, 2014), p. 20.

Theology, something which would be of use to Anglo-Catholics who might be considering engaging in church planting as part of their mission and outreach, rather than being a purely academic piece of research which would remain on a digital or library shelf. I hope therefore that this book widens the availability of this research to a constituency outside the academic community.

The work on the historical element is based on the two primary sources: biographies of the subjects of the study, Fr Richard Temple West and Mr Richard Foster. Although biographies have a danger of being oversubjective, because of the potential bias, positive or negative, of the biographer, the information they contain can often be substantiated by other documents. In the case of Temple West, there are service registers of St Mary Magdalene, Paddington accessible in the London Metropolitan Archive which confirm the claims of his biographer both in terms of offertory income and of attendance at services, as well as contemporary newspaper reports.

For Richard Foster, other corroborating information is available about the way in which he supported the building of new churches in north-east London and elsewhere, both written, particularly in the minutes of the many committees in which he was involved, and in one case, engraved on the foundation stone of St Barnabas, Walthamstow by none other than the artist Eric Gill, as well as contemporary newspaper reports. There is a wealth of other written material about the Oxford Movement and its development, and this is highlighted to set the context in which these two men worked.

The three churches which form the sites of the physical research were eventually identified via a complex network of contacts. There did not (and still does not) appear to be any one place where this information was held and certainly no network like that organized by Holy Trinity, Brompton for its Evangelical church plants. This problem is addressed in the last chapter of this book.

The three sites ranged across different stages of church planting. One in London had been well established for over ten years; the second was more recent, about five years ago. The third, in the East Midlands, began very recently. I believed that it was important to look at congregations in different stages of formation and so obtain a theoretical timeline against which to evaluate their growth, and, dare I use the word, their "success". By chance, I also stumbled on three different streams of Anglo-Catholicism.

Over a period of 18 months, I attended services monthly in each of these churches. Fortunately, the two London churches had services at different times, so I could visit both on one day. Later chapters will describe my experiences and the themes which my research has identified. Any errors or misconceptions are entirely mine. This leads to a final chapter with recommendations on how Anglo-Catholics can engage in church planting and the "church growth agenda", the language of which often seems, to many, to be quite alien.

1

Mission-Shaped Church vs the Victorians

Introduction

This chapter looks at what has been written around church planting within the Church of England over the last 30 years as well as contrasting it with Victorian activity. Although it looks at the wider Fresh Expressions agenda (of which church planting is a part), it sets it in the context of how mission is currently viewed within the Church of England. Its thrust is aimed at understanding why the Anglo-Catholic constituency in general has failed to become involved in this missional activity, and also understanding the objections which they might have in being part of such an involvement. Therefore, it considers the criticisms of the Fresh Expressions approach from theologians within the broad range of the Catholic wing of the Church of England. Given the history of the Anglo-Catholic movement, it would be expected that mission is a key part of that tradition.[1] This concept is important as the empirical research described later needs to be considered alongside current Anglo-Catholic concerns about the ecclesiological and theological validity of church planting, and the apparent lack of significant engagement resulting from those concerns. The criticisms need to be taken seriously and evaluated alongside the empirical evidence from my research.

Writing in *Mission-shaped Questions*, Angela Tilby introduces the dilemma in which Anglo-Catholics find themselves.[2] She refers to the

---

[1]   Tim Thorlby, *A Time to Sow* (London: Centre for Theology & Community, 2017), p. 88.

[2]   "What Questions Does Catholic Ecclesiology Pose for Contemporary Mission and Fresh Expressions?", in Steven J. L. Croft (ed.), *Mission-shaped*

Anglo-Catholic tradition of mission and complains that in the current climate Anglo-Catholics are very reluctant to engage with this agenda. Tilby writes about the things the tradition is good at such as liturgy, prayer and community service but contrasts that with a wide uncertainty about "giving reasons for the hope that is in us" (1 Peter 3:15). Instead she notes that Anglo-Catholics have become inward-looking, bickering and defensive.[3]

This is the context in which my empirical research took place and which I will address by engaging with other Anglo-Catholic writers and their views around Fresh Expressions and church planting. It is useful at this point to refer to Pusey's definition of Anglo-Catholicism as an indication of how most Anglo-Catholics understand the nature of the Church:

- high thoughts of the two sacraments;
- high estimate of the episcopacy as God's ordinance;
- high estimate of the visible Church as the body where we are made and continue to be members of Christ;
- regard for ordinances, as directing our devotion and disciplining us, such as daily public prayers, fasts and feasts, etc.;
- regard for the visible part of devotion, such as the decoration of the house of God, which acts insensibly on the mind;
- reverence for and defence of the ancient Church, of which our own Church is looked upon as the representative to us, and by whose views and doctrines we interpret our own Church when her meaning is questioned or doubtful; in a word, reference to the ancient Church, instead of the Reformers, as the ultimate expounder of the meaning of our Church.[4]

Questions: Defining Issues for Today's Church (London: Church House Publishing, 2008), pp. 78–9.

[3]   Steven J. L. Croft (ed.), *Mission-shaped Questions: Defining Issues for Today's Church* (London: Church House Publishing, 2008), p. 78.

[4]   Liddon, *Life of Pusey* ii, p. 140, quoted in David Edwards, *Christian England*, Vol. III (Grand Rapids, MI: William B. Eerdmans, 1984), p. 181.

Theology and church planting

Gittoes et al. highlight that innovation and inventiveness are not only a feature of the contemporary Church nor the prerogative of one part of it, but something that has existed in the Church of England throughout the last two centuries.[5] Church planting has been and continues to be an example of this. In the nineteenth century, this innovation and inventiveness engaged Evangelicals and Anglo-Catholics alike, as each in their own way sought to address both the spiritual and material needs of the growing and deprived urban population. The Anglo-Catholic "slum priests" have become part of the mythology of the nineteenth century, but they were just one element in the ways that English churches responded to the problems of cities. Alongside them were Evangelicals, both Anglican and non-conformists working to relieve poverty and need and so showing the practical nature of the gospel. In such a climate, the Salvation Army came into being along with various "settlements" in the slum areas of London.[6]

It is vital that church planting is not seen as a utilitarian or pragmatic activity, in other words, a way of proving that the local church of whatever style of churchmanship[7] is interested in mission and therefore wants to build up attendance to show its effectiveness and so be seen to be growing in purely statistical terms.[8] It needs to be grounded both in an adequate theology of mission and a rigorous ecclesiology which are true to Anglican roots. Anglo-Catholics with their high view of the nature of the Church as a continuation from the ancient Church would see anything that broke this continuity as anathema. As will be shown

---

[5] Julie Gittoes, Brutus Green, James Heard & Ian Mobsby (eds), *Generous Ecclesiology: Church, World and the Kingdom of God* (London: SCM Press, 2013), passim.

[6] Gittoes et al. (eds), *Generous Ecclesiology*, p. 25.

[7] Churchmanship is a shorthand word, used for convenience, which describes ethos, ecclesiology, style of worship and doctrinal approach.

[8] There is a tendency for churches to exaggerate their missional influence in order to prove that they are flourishing. Personal experience over 30 years of conducting archidiaconal inspections confirms this view.

later, critics of Fresh Expressions take issue both with its theology and ecclesiology. Andrew Davison and Alison Milbank make this clear in the opening words of *For the Parish*. They claim that *Mission-shaped* Church is ecclesiologically flawed. They claim that it shapes the ecclesiology of the Church of England in spite of its theological and philosophical flaws.[9]

Why theology and ecclesiology matter

Alister McGrath importantly highlights the centrality of theology and doctrine in church growth:

> Theology matters to church growth, precisely because it aims to sustain the luminous and captivating vision of God which lies at the heart of the Christian faith, defending it against well-meaning attempts to reduce it to something manageable and culturally accessible, which ultimately robs it of its depth and vitality.[10]

This is a particular concern for the Anglo-Catholics. Angela Tilby stresses the theological importance of history for an Anglo-Catholic understanding of Church and mission.[11] She sees the Church as "the mission of God extending through time". In Anglicanism, it is through liturgy and sacrament that this continuity is expressed and so forms the theological foundation for its ecclesiology. Any church planting activity needs to take seriously the issue of theology and it is in this respect that the different methods involved in Practical Theology are particularly useful. Practical Theology takes its starting point from a given real situation and

---

[9]   Andrew Davison and Alison Milbank, *For the Parish: A Critique of Fresh Expressions* (London: SCM Press, 2010), p. 1.

[10] In David Goodhew, *Towards a Theology of Church Growth* (Farnham: Ashgate, 2015), pp. 93–106.

[11] "What Questions Does Catholic Ecclesiology Pose for Contemporary Mission and Fresh Expressions?", in Steven J. L. Croft (ed.), *Mission-shaped Questions: Defining Issues for Today's Church* (London: Church House Publishing, 2008), p. 79.

analyses it using various methods, drawn from a range of theories both in the arts and in science, but interpreted within a theological framework.[12]

A unique mark of Anglican identity is the historic episcopate. Tilby draws on Clement of Rome in 96 CE to emphasize the role of the bishop in mission.[13] A proper relationship with the diocesan bishop is essential, for through the bishop a church is linked to the wider church and so can claim to be a part of the one, holy Catholic and apostolic church. *Breaking New Ground* is quite clear on this:

> The Episcopate represents the church's catholicity. In summary, unless a church plant offered on a regular basis the dominical sacraments and had a good relationship with and the active support of the diocesan bishop, Anglo-Catholics would not accept that it was an authentic expression of church.[14]

What has happened since 1994

As a response to various "unofficial" church plants, often in parishes with no relationship to the "planting church", in 1994 the House of Bishops commissioned the report, quoted above, *Breaking New Ground*.[15] This report aimed to highlight good practice as well as to address some of the problems caused by these unauthorized plants. The significance of this report is that for the first time, church planting was recognized by the Church of England as a legitimate strategy for mission. In 2002, the Church of England Board of Mission set up a group to review this report.

---

[12] Richard Robert Osmer, *Practical Theology: An Introduction* (Grand Rapids, MI: William B. Eerdmans, 2008), p. 4.

[13] Tilby, "What Questions Does Catholic Ecclesiology Pose for Contemporary Mission and Fresh Expressions?", pp. 78–89.

[14] *Breaking New Ground: Church Planting in the Church of England* (London: Church House Publishing, 1994), p. 3.

[15] *Breaking New Ground*, passim.

This group published its report, *Mission-Shaped Church* (*MSC*) in 2004.[16] In the same year, Steven Croft, at the time Warden of Cranmer Hall in St John's College, Durham (and later to become Bishop of Sheffield and subsequently Oxford), was appointed as Archbishops' Missioner and leader of Fresh Expressions. He was followed in this role in 2009 by Bishop Graham Cray, who had chaired the working group that produced *MSC*.

Mission-Shaped Church—The Report

The foreword to this report, written by the then Archbishop of Canterbury, Dr Rowan Williams, clearly sets the agenda:

> [W]e have begun to realize that there are many ways in which the reality of 'church' can exist. 'Church' as a map of territorial divisions (parishes and dioceses) is one—one that still has remarkable vigour in all sorts of contexts and which relates to a central conviction about the vocation of Anglicanism. But there are more and more others, of the kind that this report describes and examines. The challenge is not to force everything into the familiar mould; but neither is it to tear up the rulebook and start from scratch (as if that were ever possible or realistic).[17]

Bishop Graham Cray in his introduction refers to the changing nature of communities and hence the need for the Church to be responsive to this if it is to fulfil the Anglican incarnational principle.[18] The division of the Church of England into parishes, which had begun in Saxon times, means that each part of England is the responsibility of its parish priest. The incarnational principle of the Church mirrors the incarnation of

---

16   Mission and Public Affairs Council, *Mission-Shaped Church: Church Planting and Fresh Expressions of Church in a Changing Context* (London: Church House Publishing, 2004).

17   *MSC*, p. vii.

18   I refer to this later as being crucial for Anglo-Catholic ecclesiology.

Jesus, "The word was made flesh and pitched his tent among us."[19] Just as Jesus lived among the people of his day the parish priest should mirror this. This principle is enshrined in the Canon Law of the Church of England which states that the incumbent must live in their vicarage with the parish.

Even today, many vicarages are adjacent to the parish church or in some cases physically attached to it.[20] Therefore, the practical result of this Canon is that in many parishes, especially in inner cities, the priest is now the only "professional" who actually lives in the parish. This principle, that the incumbent resides in the parsonage house of the benefice, is important and is vital for Anglo-Catholics who might want to consider church planting, as it negates the view that a Fresh Expression or a church plant is divorced from its founding parish.[21] As will be shown later, critics of MSC and Fresh Expressions often assume, in many cases wrongly, a disconnect between the parish and the mission initiative.

Thus, the report maintains that there is no single standard form of church which can any longer meet the needs of the diverse cultures, although it insists that the parochial system is still a vital part of the way in which the Church of England delivers its mission. It is worth emphasizing this as a number of critics have accused MSC of undermining the parish system.[22] One must also consider at this time definitions of terms as used in MSC, as it stresses both the importance of Fresh Expressions and of church planting; church planting and Fresh Expressions of church can

---

[19] John 1:14 (my translation).

[20] The vicarage in my own parish, a Victorian replacement of an older house, is adjacent to the church and accessible via the churchyard. Many Victorian Anglo-Catholic churches either had the clergy house attached or within the curtilage of the church as is the case with St Barnabas, Walthamstow, where the vicarage door is opposite the north door of the church, separated by a path about three yards wide.

[21] When we were considering planting a new church in my current parish, the first thing we did, jointly with the diocese, was to buy a house right in the middle of the new housing development.

[22] For example, see Davison and Milbank, *For the Parish*.

have similar origins and similar aims. They are different but are related and both are important for the Church's mission.[23]

MSC identifies 12 types of Fresh Expressions.[24] Michael Moynagh uses the metaphor of a journey to describe church planting.[25] He identifies two forms: a "worship-first" journey and a "serving-first journey". In the worship-first journey, a congregation from an existing large church is planted into another area, often into a church threatened with closure. The aim is to preserve and strengthen the existing congregation. The serving-first journey starts within a given community. A local church believes there is some need within a particular part of its parish. First it tries to listen (perhaps through visiting campaigns, open meetings, or questionnaires) to identify that particular need and then respond to it in some way. Given the tradition of social action within Anglo-Catholicism, this route might be thought to be attractive to such churches as their preferred method of mission. Both journeys fit within the definition of church planting suggested in *MSC* whereby the mission of the church is embedded in a particular context to bring to faith new disciples.[26] As will be seen later, it is important to plan exactly what is the desired outcome.

Mission-Shaped Church—its underpinning theology

MSC devotes a chapter to "Theology for a Missionary Church".[27] It sees mission as derived from the nature of the relationships within the Trinity and in fact speaks of "the mission of God" (*missio Dei*—the sending of/by God). The giving of the Spirit is linked with the sending of the apostles into the world: "As the Father has sent me, I am sending you."[28]

---

[23]   *MSC*, p. 34.

[24]   *MSC*, p. 44.

[25]   Michael Moynagh with Philip Harrold, *Church for Every Context: An Introduction to Theology and Practice* (London: SCM Press, 2012), pp. 206–21.

[26]   *MSC*, p. 32.

[27]   *MSC*, pp. 84–102.

[28]   John 20:21.

Mission, therefore, is understood as being derived from the very nature of God. So, it sits within the context of the doctrine of the Trinity, not as one might expect, within that of ecclesiology or soteriology because the doctrine of the nature of God is foundational since the rest of Christian doctrine springs from it. Key to the outworking of *missio Dei* is the doctrine of the incarnation. *MSC* emphasizes this by stating that the incarnation took place at a particular historical time in a specific geographical location and in a particular culture.[29]

Angela Tilby, from her Anglo-Catholic standpoint, is concerned about how the Church as part of the *missio Dei* retains its continuity through time.[30] She sees Fresh Expressions as a bridge into the Church. This may be applicable to some church plants but not to all, for, as will be seen later, some, by her own definition, are churches in their own right.[31] Critics of *MSC*, especially Andrew Davison and Alison Milbank, strongly object to what they see as its segregationist emphasis which can be seen as antithetical to the concept of the social Trinity.[32] Pete Ward writes: "Debates around the Trinity, for instance, have incorporated notions of relationship and community as central to their themes", and he cites a number of theologians in support of this statement.[33] So any tendency towards segregation militates against the concepts of relationship and community which are essential elements of the application of the doctrine of the Trinity to present-day church life.

Such criticisms will be covered in more depth later, but they show the tensions that can arise in any planning for a church plant or new congregation. Is the new church aimed at reaching and engaging those within a particular cultural or social group or covering a particular geographic area (which in turn could also have cultural implications)? Quoting Donald McGavran, *MSC* concedes that this is probably "one of the most contentious issues that arise in connection with church

---

[29]   *MSC*, p. 87.

[30]   In Croft, *Mission-Shaped Questions*, p. 88.

[31]   *Croft, Mission-Shaped Questions*, p. 79.

[32]   Davison and Milbank, *For the Parish*, pp. 64–92.

[33]   Pete Ward, *Introducing Practical Theology: Mission, Ministry, and the Life of the Church* (Grand Rapids, MI: Baker Academic, 2017), p. 123.

planting".[34] McGavran posited what he called the Homogeneous Unit Principle. He believed and evidenced, from his mission field experience in India in the first half of the twentieth century, that people who became Christians did not want to move out of their culture, class, caste groups; they were more comfortable with people "like themselves". It is possible to find scriptural support both for and against this principle, but it is important to recognize the huge gap both in culture and time that exists since McGavran proposed this theory. Nevertheless, those who are engaged in church planting need to have a very clear rationale of what they are trying to achieve and whom they are aiming to reach, underpinned by a coherent theology within the demographic and cultural milieu in which they work. In Luke 14:28ff., Jesus uses illustrations of building a tower or preparing for war as reminders of the cost of discipleship and the need to ensure that all the relevant issues are properly considered. His emphasis on proper planning and preparation serves to underline the importance of the approach outlined above, from a theological stance as well as from a more practical position. So, Anglo-Catholics would look at any suggestions of starting a church plant, not only from the physical practicalities but also how such an activity would enhance the mission of the church through the ministry of word and sacrament. This concept is referred to in later chapters as "intentionality".

Recent literature about current Anglo-Catholic church planting

The literature around current church planting and especially Anglo-Catholic activity is relatively sparse. The Centre for Theology & Community published a report, *Love, Sweat and Tears*, in 2016.[35] The report is the first fully researched and published account of church planting undertaken in East London through the Holy Trinity Brompton

---

[34] *MSC*, p. 108.

[35] The Centre for Theology & Community, *Love, Sweat and Tears: Church Planting in East London* (London: 2016). <http://www.theology-centre.org.uk/resources/research/>, accessed 18 January 2023.

(HTB) Network. It relates the experience of five existing churches, of a range of churchmanship, which have benefited from planting over the ten-year period from 2005–15, beginning with St Paul's, Shadwell. The Diocese of London prefers the term "church graft" when involving existing congregations.

As far as this research into Anglo-Catholic church planting is concerned, the most significant of these studies relates to that of St Peter's Bethnal Green. This was an Anglo-Catholic parish which was declining and has been revived by church planting, as HTB had been approached by the PCC to come in and offer support. It is significant to note that the traditional 10 a.m. Holy Communion has been maintained, with a Sung Eucharist, usually monthly. The parish describes itself on its website:

> At St Peter's we're a "cross-tradition" Anglican church, so we **worship God** in many styles, encountering God through the **scriptures**, the **sacraments** and the **Spirit**.[36]

The report ends by stating that any revival in the church's fortunes will need a variety of approaches. Church planting is not a cure-all but has a role to play and can be undertaken within existing church structures.

The other significant report, again from The Centre for Theology & Community, is *A Time to Sow*.[37] Although its aim is to describe growing Anglo-Catholic parishes, its final section puts that growth into perspective and addresses Anglo-Catholic church planting—or rather the lack of it.[38] Tim Thorlby identifies the drive for Evangelical church growth and planting with the leadership and support of a handful of large churches which have also encouraged plants to become involved in the supportive networks which they have set up.[39] He was not able to identify any Anglo-Catholic church that was currently undertaking such a role. Given the history of Anglo-Catholic church planting, particularly in the nineteenth century, he sees it as strange that there is such a lack

---

[36] <http://www.stpetersbethnalgreen.org/worship/>, accessed 18 January 2023.

[37] Thorlby, *A Time to Sow*.

[38] Thorlby, *A Time to Sow*, pp. 83–91.

[39] <https://www.htb.org/network>, accessed 18 January 2023.

of willingness to do so today. In Walthamstow in 1840, there was one Anglican church; by 1911 there were 18, mainly Anglo-Catholic, funded in part or in whole by the generosity and theological zeal of Richard Foster (1822–1910).[40] Thorlby contrasts the enthusiasm for mission that led to the building of these churches with what he sees as happening in Anglo-Catholic circles today. He concludes:

> [T]he tradition's profound understanding of the importance of incarnational ministry and the rootedness of its worship in age-old truths is surely more relevant than ever in a city typified by constant change and rootlessness. Yet it is clear that the tradition has a challenge on its hands to recover the vision and energy it once had for growth and mission.[41]

This comment illustrates how slowly Anglo-Catholic churches have moved in the past ten years, in spite of the national drive towards church growth and church planting. Steven Croft wrote in 2009 that he believed that Fresh Expressions had "theological integrity" across all parts of the Church of England.[42]

David Goodhew and Anthony-Paul Cooper's jointly edited *The Desecularisation of the City* shows the changes that have taken place in church life and the formation/planting of new churches in London across many denominations and it includes a digest of Thorlby's work.[43] There is also a useful chapter by Bob Jackson on the trends within the Anglican Church in London since 1980 which highlight numerical growth in parishes as well as the establishment of church plants.[44]

---

[40]   Steven Saxby, *Anglican Church Building in Victorian Walthamstow* (London: Walthamstow Historical Society, 2014), pp. 3–4.

[41]   Thorlby, *A Time to Sow*, p. 91.

[42]   Steven Croft and Ian Mobsby (eds), *Fresh Expressions in the Sacramental Tradition* (Norwich: Canterbury Press, 2009), p. 50.

[43]   David Goodhew and Anthony-Paul Cooper (eds), *The Desecularisation of the City: London's Churches, 1980 to the Present* (Abingdon: Routledge, 2019).

[44]   Goodhew and Cooper, *Desecularisation*, pp. 262–80.

Criticisms of *MSC* and its approach

Since the publication of *MSC*, there has been a significant number of books, articles and pamphlets published, aiming to substantiate or evidence its conclusions, as well as others which set out to challenge the underlying basis and assumptions of Fresh Expressions and church planting. This section describes the criticism of *MSC* by a number of, mainly academic, theologians and is offered to balance what is written in *MSC* and advocated by those involved in church planting. Any church that is considering a plant should look at these criticisms and see how relevant they might be for their situation.

The strongest of these criticisms is *For the Parish* (*FTP*).[45] The authors, Andrew Davison and Alison Milbank, both stand as academics as well as ordained clergy in the Anglo-Catholic tradition. Philosophically, *MSC* is accused of separating form and content, so that the metaphors of clothing and fashion, used frequently in *MSC*, imply that the rejection of outward forms does not destroy the content of the gospel. Davison and Milbank object to this concept as, along with the idea of choice of denominations, they see it as a matter of style. They hold strongly to the view that the Church of England is not simply one denomination among many, because of not only its history but also its legal status as the Established Church, which differentiates it in its governance and position from all other churches. They see the historic place of a parish with its parish church as the key to mission and as such believe it to be undermined by Fresh Expressions and church plants. They state that Fresh Expressions only meet one situation, whereas "the inherited church" has faced and can continue to face a variety of situations. They believe that the parish church can adapt to meet new challenges.[46]

Much of the criticism made by Davison and Milbank is influenced by their view of the make-up of the working group that produced *MSC*. The members were all involved in some form of parish ministry or held diocesan managerial roles for ministerial or mission support. Davison and Milbank decry the absence of academic theologians in the membership

---

45   Davison and Milbank, *For the Parish*.

46   Davison and Milbank, *For the Parish*, p. 9.

of this working party and name a number of those whom they believe should have been involved. This view colours much of the rest of their analysis.[47] Yet they criticize the useful analytical and theological tool of the Pastoral Cycle.[48] In the understanding of Davison and Milbank, Fresh Expressions appears to have developed in a vacuum, divorced from the life of a parish. This is far from the case as most such activities are run by loyal church members, with the blessing and encouragement, usually combined with financial support, of incumbents and church councils, and more frequently than not, within the boundaries of the existing parish. Yet the underlying theme of *FTP* seems to be that there is a divorce between Fresh Expressions and traditional parish life rather than seeing it as another way of developing the mission of the parish.

A significant part of the book relates to mission and particularly how it relates to modern culture, which they perceive as one of the reasons for the concept of Fresh Expressions. Davison and Milbank see it as a response to a consumer-driven society and hence the introduction of an element of choice in the way people might want to meet their spiritual needs. However, there is a significant lack of empirical evidence to back up this claim. What evidence they offer is anecdotal and concentrated on what might be classed as unusual or extreme examples, like "the book group", the "card-making church", or the "knitting group church". They manifestly fail to acknowledge that informal groups are, and always have been, legitimate ways of introducing people into the social life of a church as a bridge towards an understanding of and an encounter with the gospel. The journey to faith is a very varied one, and it is invidious to criticize techniques that are being used to help people make that journey. Such methods echo what St Paul wrote: "I have become all things to all people, so that by any means I might save some" (1 Corinthians 9:22). Churches have always had separate interest groups and some people never "progress" from them into full worshipping church life. The problem with making such a criticism is that one could be left needing to castigate traditional and long-established groups such as women's fellowships, the Mothers' Union, men's groups or other similar activities,

---

47   Davison and Milbank, *For the Parish*, p. 225.

48   Davison and Milbank, *For the Parish*, p. 128.

which many people see as "their church". It might be, however, that the criticisms of *FTP* are only of those that are formally badged as Fresh Expressions and therefore often labelled as "church" in order to tick a box on an official form.[49] Therefore, Davison and Milbank see the lack within many Fresh Expressions of the formal structures of worship—the formal preaching of the Word and the administration of the sacraments—as a significant negative approach to mission compared with that played by the historic role of the parish church—"A Christian Presence in Every Community", as the Church of England describes itself.

A response to criticisms of *MSC*

The criticisms of *MSC* and activities that flow from it, by Davison and Milbank, would be easier to accept if they were based on solid empirical data about the vitality of the traditional parish church. These criticisms, together with what seems a break with the historical tradition, have led many Anglo-Catholics to regard any form of Fresh Expression and church planting as not something with which they wish to engage. As will be seen later, there are parishes in which church planting is taking place and lessons can be learned from these. Davison and Milbank write: "Sociology is allowed to triumph over theology."[50] Such an analysis leads them to deny the suggestion, which they see, in my view incorrectly, as being implicit in *MSC*, that the Church is just another voluntary organization among many others, whereas it is "the Body of Christ and the bearer of his mission in the world".[51]

---

[49] The Annual Statistics for Mission Form that parishes are asked to complete has a question about Fresh Expressions. When conducting church inspections on behalf of the archdeacon for more than 30 years, I have seen many of these forms, and what I would regard as normal parish activities are often included—probably to show to "The Diocese" that a parish is engaged in the Fresh Expressions agenda.

[50] Davison and Milbank, *For the Parish*, p. 80.

[51] Davison and Milbank, *For the Parish*, p. 81.

The only evidence on which these criticisms are based is a short, generalized statement about the parish church and its historical links with its community, whereas those of us who have been involved in the wider pastoral and missional oversight of a diocese in many cases see things very differently. There is an obvious gap in *For the Parish* between the theological critique and an understanding of the realities of much of parish ministry. The Mission and Pastoral Measure 2011 made reorganization of parishes a much easier process.[52] This has resulted in the creation of many more multi-parish benefices in order to ensure that resources (both human and financial) are used in a much more efficient way. The monochrome and optimistic view of the role of the parish and its life, described by Davison and Milbank, is very hard to evidence in the life of today's church and serves to reveal the gap between their theological critique and an understanding of the realities of much of parish ministry. If their belief about the parish were grounded in what is happening in the 16,000 or so parishes that make up the Church of England, there would be no need for Fresh Expressions nor any other type of mission initiative; all would be well and thriving. They see the parish itself as being the centre of mission, culture and Christian education.[53] Sadly this is not always the case and reports such as *From Anecdote to Evidence* as well as the annual statistics published centrally by the Church of England provide the evidence for this. In many parishes, both rural and urban, the church is seen to be beleaguered and demoralized. Clergy, particularly in rural areas, have an increasing number of parishes to oversee, and they minister to a diminishing number of active and ageing worshippers as the Annual Statistics for Mission for 2018 evidence:

> The total Worshipping Community of churches across the
> Church of England in 2018 was 1.12 million people, of whom

---

[52]   Church of England, *Mission and Pastoral Measure 2011*, <https://www.churchofengland.org/resources/parish-reorganisation-and-church-property/mission-and-pastoral-measure-2011-and-code>, accessed 18 January 2023.

[53]   Davison and Milbank, *For the Parish*, p. 169.

20% were aged under 18, 48% were aged 18–69, and 33% were aged 70 or over.[54]

The figures for 2021 (published as this book was being drafted) show an even more bleak picture. The total Worshipping Community was 966,000 people, of whom 17 per cent were aged under 18, 46.6 per cent were aged 18–69 and 36.4 per cent were aged 70 or over.[55]

The current agenda, therefore, is often one of church retrenchment rather than church planting and growth. Even where there is the opportunity to reduce clergy work pressures, like joint PCCs in a multi-parish benefice, these opportunities are rarely grasped because of a reluctance to accept change.[56] On this subject, Evelyn Underhill wrote as far back as 1936:

> Departure from the ordained routine always produces a feeling of discomfort, and usually arouses hostility; as anyone well knows who has tried to introduce 'desirable changes' into the worship of an English village church.[57]

The comments of Davison and Milbank about choice, which they see MSC as advocating, are also ill-considered. It is worth at this point

---

[54]   Church of England, *Statistics for Mission,* <https://www.churchofengland. org/about/research-and-statistics/key-areas-research#church-attendance-statistics>, accessed 18 January 2023.

[55]   Church of England, *Statistics for Mission,* <https://www.churchofengland. org/system/files/private%3A//2022–12///2021StatisticsForMission.pdf>, accessed 18 January 2023.

[56]   David Pytches tells the story of a visit Archbishop Robert Runcie made to a parish, just after becoming Bishop of St Albans. He met an elderly churchwarden who had held that position for over 30 years. The bishop remarked to the churchwarden that he must have seen many changes. The response was "Indeed I have, bishop, and I have resisted every one of them." In N. A. D. Scotland (ed.), *Recovering the Ground* (Chorleywood: Kingdom Power Trust Publications, 1995), p. 22.

[57]   Evelyn Underhill, *Worship* (London: Nisbet & Co. Ltd, 1936), p. 34.

noting that choice has always been the case in larger towns and cities, whereby people attend the Anglican (or other) church which is more sympathetic to their theology or preferred style of worship rather than the parish church where they live, as would have been the case in earlier centuries with far less ease of travel. In London, does one attend All Souls, Langham Place or All Saints, Margaret Street? St Helen's Bishopsgate or Holy Redeemer, Clerkenwell? This is choice based on a number of different factors, not just a simple preference but with underlying issues of theology, aesthetics, style of preaching, forms of liturgy, type of building, to name but a few. At the beginning of the twentieth century, Charles Booth commented: "But most people simply seek the kind of service that suits them, wherever it might be found within range."[58] As can be seen, such choice is not new.

Davison and Milbank's optimistic vision of the role of the parish is to be commended, but it is at variance with much of the reality that those of us involved in parish ministry encounter on a daily basis. It appears more like a "Platonic form of parish" than what a parish is like in reality. The book does raise serious questions which those involved in or considering church planting need to recognize and consider, but its general message is too negative, so it does not support the Church's mission in the challenging environment of the twenty-first century.

It is these kinds of perceptions that have made the whole Fresh Expressions movement (and I include church planting in this) seem alien to Anglo-Catholics. The continuity of the Church, expressed in the concept of Apostolic Succession from New Testament times, was one of the key features of the Oxford Movement and still remains important for today's Anglo-Catholics. Fresh Expressions can appear to put this continuity at risk by divorcing a form of mission activity from the wider sacramental life of the Church and thereby setting up what can seem to be an informal and competing system. This can lead to the negative criticisms such as can be seen in *For the Parish*. Other parts of the Church of England sit more lightly on this concept of historic continuity and the sacramental life and therefore seem willing to adopt a more flexible and

---

[58]   Charles Booth, *Life and Labour of the People in London, 3rd Series: Religious Influences* (London: Macmillan & Co. Ltd, 1902), Volume 7, p. 4.

informal approach. However, this continuity is the core of Anglicanism. A. M. Ramsey put it like this:

> What is there then in the contemporary world which has continuity and identity with the pure church of antiquity? In continuity, the Anglican church is his [John Henry Newman's] answer, for he sees a real continuity in belief, sacramental order, also in the supernatural life between the Anglican church in principle and the primitive church.[59]

This statement of Ramsey's encapsulates Anglo-Catholic thinking about how Anglicanism is seen as being in continuity with the primitive church, the last point of Pusey's definition already referred to.[60]

A similar critique is made by Martyn Percy, who has often been a critic of managerialism and the introduction of "business-speak" into the life of the Church.[61] This position underpins many of his strictures around Fresh Expressions, especially in Chapter 4 of *Shaping the Church*.[62] Percy's criticisms look at the way in which Fresh Expressions have developed. He sees the concept as part of a continuum of initiatives that have occurred, particularly in the Evangelical charismatic wing of the Church of England, over the last few decades—but an initiative which, this time, carries the approval of General Synod and hence episcopal support and approval, backed by finance, in virtually every diocese.[63]

Percy's critique, in essence, is that Fresh Expressions is part of the packaging of the Christian message into marketing terms to fit in with modern ideas of choice, newness and cultural relevance, what might be

---

[59]   A. M. Ramsey, "John Henry Newman and the Oxford Movement", *Anglican and Episcopal History* 59:3 (September 1990), pp. 330–44.

[60]   In David Edwards, *Christian England*, Vol. III, p. 181. Original in Liddon, *Life of Pusey* ii, p. 140.

[61]   Martyn Percy, "Growth and management in the Church of England: some comments", *Modern Believing* 55 (2014), pp. 257–70.

[62]   Martyn Percy, *Shaping the Church: The Promise of Implicit Theology* (Farnham: Ashgate, 2010).

[63]   Percy, *Shaping the Church*, p. 73.

termed as "commodifying the gospel".[64] He challenges the idea that "new" is better than "old" and sees Fresh Expressions as a way of avoiding some of the current complexities and difficulties of church involvement. Rather in his view, they "mirror contemporary secular preoccupations: with pragmatism, growth, freshness, alternatives and newness".[65] He agrees that Fresh Expressions make some positive contribution to church life but only a small one. He sees the Church with its structure of parishes, deaneries and archdeaconries within a diocese as fundamental to this. He recognizes the value in this traditional system which links different types of churches across a relatively small area into Area or Rural Deaneries and so enables the provision of a variety of ministry. However, like Davison and Milbank and their view of the parish, his vision of "deanery" is, in my experience, a very idealistic one, which does not always hold true in reality. It might be true of an urban deanery which just covers one whole town, e.g., Luton, and so has some sort of natural focus and cohesion, but many deaneries, just like many parliamentary constituencies, are much more diverse and lack a focal centre; they are just a collection of parishes which occupy a geographical area which can be delineated on a map to make up a reasonable population total.[66] He sums up his views by stating that if the Church were to disappear, there would be left a multi-choice menu of spirituality which is insufficient to maintain the faith.[67]

Although not within the Anglo-Catholic constituency and also with a contradictory ecclesiology of being an Anglican layperson but also a URC elder, the views of John Hull have some resonance to the Anglo-Catholic views expressed by Percy, Davison and Milbank. There is some divergence but his concept of Deuteronomic self-fulfilling prophecy has validity, as he sees Fresh Expressions and church planting as panic-driven

---

[64]   Percy, *Shaping the Church*, p. 70.

[65]   Percy, *Shaping the Church*, p. 78.

[66]   I write from first-hand experience, having been a deanery lay co-chair for over 30 years of a quite disparate deanery. Sadly, this approach is seemingly being adopted by the Boundary Commission for parliamentary constituencies. <https://www.bcereviews.org.uk/>, accessed 18 January 2023.

[67]   Percy, *Shaping the Church*, p. 78.

initiatives to make the Church relevant to today's culture and so keep it alive. Angela Tilby raises the same sort of question when she asks:

> But am I wrong sometimes to discern in fresh expressions thinking an itchy restlessness which itself may be a product of our media-saturated consumerist culture? . . . Have we just become too good at identifying people's needs and producing a version of the gospel that apparently meets the need, but fails to transform it?[68]

The concerns raised by Davison and Milbank as well as by Martyn Percy are based on their understanding of what the Church is and the place of the Church of England within it as well as an objection to what they see as a purely sociological response to mission. These writers share a vision of the Church that is one, holy, Catholic and apostolic and see in Fresh Expressions a watering down of this description in favour of novelty and choice. They stress the continuity of liturgy and worship which is the essence of Anglicanism. They decry what they see as a "pick and mix" approach to worship and church life. "The risk for 'Catholic' Fresh Expressions is that 'Catholic practice' is seen as and becomes a box of odds and ends."[69] Because Catholic practices are employed outside of their traditional and structured liturgical context, they become devoid of their underlying meaning and so lack substance and, in reality, become purely decorative. As will be seen later, Victorian commentators had similar concerns about ritual for the sake of ritual.

The church growth agenda

An important question that now needs to be raised is how Anglo-Catholics understand "church growth" and whether it is part of their ecclesiology. The Victorians built new churches as a response to growing urbanization. How does this relate to Anglo-Catholics today?

---

68   In Croft (ed.), *Mission-shaped Questions*, p. 87.
69   Croft (ed.), *Mission-shaped Questions*, p. 109.

The incarnational principle embodied in the parish system emphasizes place, and together with the view of historic continuity already referred to, this is part of the Anglo-Catholic mindset. The significance of good liturgy is also an important factor. There is also the element of serving the community which in the past fired much of Anglo-Catholic mission. One would therefore expect that church planting would be as important an element in current Anglo-Catholic mission as it was in the Victorian era.

An important contribution to church growth literature is *Church for Every Context*, co-authored by Michael Moynagh and Philip Harrold. Chapter 11 describes a process by which those who are involved in church planting can best achieve their objectives. Moynagh offers a theological interpretation by reflecting on Luke's account of the ministry of Jesus, although his interpretation is open to a number of questions as the process that he claims to see in the gospel narrative is nowhere near as obviously linear as he asserts. He concludes this chapter by commending a "serving-first journey" for three reasons, in that it helps to clarify the strategy and what is put in place to implement it; it emphasizes the role of the community rather than "churchiness"; and finally, it brings to the forefront the love of neighbour, so important in Jesus's teaching, rather than seeing people as objects for conversion. This serving model should commend itself to Anglo-Catholics, but its rejection of "churchiness" could well be a barrier for those who see worship as a way of bringing the community into a relationship with God. "Both ... and" rather than "either ... or" might seem more acceptable. The Victorian Anglo-Catholics placed equal value on the beauty of worship as well as their social service. Peter Doll writes: "Ritualism is a sort of excursion train on Sunday, to bring the poor man out of his dull, squalid, every-day life into a land of beauty, colour, light and song."[70] Even if Anglo-Catholic mythology has exaggerated the influence of the slum missions, the moral imperative and spirit of sacrifice that priests and religious brought to their work and worship were nevertheless genuine and powerful.[71]

---

[70] In Stewart J. Brown (ed.), *The Oxford Handbook of the Oxford Movement* (Oxford: Oxford University Press, 2017).

[71] John Shelton Reed, *Glorious Battle: The Cultural Politics of Victorian Anglo-Catholicism* (Nashville, TN: Nashville University Press, 1996), p. 150.

In his introduction to Moynagh and Harrold's book, Steven Croft expresses the hope that the essays contained will be of benefit and support for all engaged in church planting.[72] One of the key drivers identified is a phrase originally used by Rowan Williams when he was Archbishop of Wales—"a mixed economy church".[73] By this he meant that traditional forms of church based on the parish system and the parish church should co-exist with different and new ways of "being church", whether it be a new type of activity or a newly established worshipping community. This can be seen as an extension of what happens in practice, particularly in a large church. So, there is already in place some form of a mixed economy. Any new Fresh Expression would merely widen the available choices.[74]

Mission-shaped Questions devotes a significant number of its chapters to exploring the nature and role of the Church especially in regard to Fresh Expressions. Importantly it looks at some of the ecclesiological issues regarding church order, sacramental worship and the relationship of the Church to current culture and society; in other words it aims to link the theory with the reality of church life. Croft sums up the challenge that faces the Church in its mission by emphasizing the need for the best theological and other resources to be available to those engaged in church planting—or any other form of Fresh Expression.

Another recent important piece of thinking around church growth of which church planting is one of the essential elements is *Towards a Theology of Church Growth* published in 2015.[75] It contains contributions

---

[72] Moynagh and Harrold, *Church for Every Context*, p. x.

[73] Croft (ed.), *Mission-shaped Questions*, p. 26. This is a phrase from the introduction to a report *Good News in Wales*, p. 3. The full quotation is: "We may discern signs of hope [in Wales]. These may be found particularly in the development of a mixed economy of church life . . . There are ways of being church alongside the inherited parochial pattern."

[74] As an example, in my own liberal Catholic parish, a monthly "Messy Mass" has extended the reach of All-age Communion to those who want an even more informal style of worship, and this has now been further augmented by a quarterly "Forest Church" in which the involvement with the physical world as created by God can be seen as a door to the Kingdom.

[75] Goodhew (ed.), *Towards a Theology of Church Growth*.

from a number of theologians from across the different traditions of
the Church of England; it therefore cannot be accused of being biased
towards any one type of theology or churchmanship. It is important
also to recognize that any form of church growth must include the idea
of planting new churches, as well as looking at ways in which existing
congregations can grow. In his introduction, Goodhew states:

> The volume argues that the numerical growth of the church
> should be of central concern for churches and individual
> Christians. But it also seeks to guard against ill-thought-out
> justifications of church growth which draw less from theology
> than from pragmatic notions of what constitutes 'success'.[76]

He emphasizes that growth is a wide concept that includes, but not
exclusively, the numerical. He quotes some words from an address of
Rowan Williams to the General Synod of the Church of England in
November 2010 in which he proposed a three-fold definition of growth:
personal holiness, the transformation of society and the numerical
growth of church congregations.[77] While accepting the validity of this
definition, Goodhew intends to focus particularly on numerical growth
as he agrees that there is a need to challenge some of the assumptions
that are commonly made, which are critical of the idea of looking at
numerical growth.

The first part of the introduction pulls out the main themes of each
of the subsequent chapters, using particularly significant quotations,
and so is a very helpful pointer for what is to follow and enables the
reader to concentrate on specific areas of interest. He then engages in
a "questioning of church growth in the context of late modernity".[78] He
maintains that the idea of context is problematic and reflects as much
on the context of the research theologian as on the context of any given
church. Goodhew maintains that the Church is trapped in a theology
of decline, leading to a self-fulfilling prophecy. This echoes John Hull's

---

[76]   Goodhew (ed.), *Towards a Theology of Church Growth*, p. 3.

[77]   Goodhew (ed.), *Towards a Theology of Church Growth*, p. 5.

[78]   Goodhew (ed.), *Towards a Theology of Church Growth*, p. 27.

critique in *Mission-Shaped Church: A Theological Response*.[79] Goodhew would want to stress an alternative view, that the local congregation is of value and has a significant role to play in the bringing to life of the Kingdom of God. The values of the Kingdom, enshrined in neighbourly love in all its individual and communal aspects, need vibrant and lively local congregations to reflect these values. This statement is one that should be welcomed by Anglo-Catholics as it incorporates the incarnational principle of "place" and links it both with worship and service, so again mirroring what was happening in the nineteenth century when new Anglo-Catholic churches were being built. Goodhew believes that by developing a clear theology around church growth, there will be a place for considering numerical growth as real evidence of the building of the Kingdom of God.[80] In this way, the church with an emphasis on growth can challenge the secular western culture, rather than adopting a strategy of growth as merely a pragmatic act of desperation in the face of an apparent continued decline.[81]

As far as official follow-up of church growth/planting issues is concerned, *From Anecdote to Evidence* was published in 2014 as a report of a two-year research programme between 2011 and 2013 looking at why churches grow (or do not).[82] Pages 17–19 summarize the research on church planting. Twenty-seven plants were researched qualitatively, with several different models investigated, mostly centred around worship. Nearly all of the models originated from charismatic or traditional Evangelical churches, and as such are moulded by this, both theologically and ecclesiologically. However, there is reference to an Anglo-Catholic model with reference to churches planted and supported by parish churches within their own parishes. It encourages further consideration about the meaning of church planting in an Anglo-Catholic context.[83]

---

[79] John M. Hull, *Mission-Shaped Church: A Theological Response* (London: SCM Press, 2006), p. 20.

[80] Goodhew, *Shaping the Church*, p. 35.

[81] Goodhew, *Shaping the Church*, p. 33.

[82] *From Anecdote to Evidence.*

[83] *From Anecdote to Evidence*, p. 19.

The report quotes the Revd Dr Graham Tomlin, later Bishop of Kensington, as saying that what makes church plants grow is the quality of ordained leadership.[84] This is particularly true in Anglo-Catholic church plants where the report notes a comment by an Anglo-Catholic priest with a church plant that "Catholics are not affirmed in church planting" and "there is no support for Catholic initiatives in church planting".[85] So the ordained leaders believe that they are left in isolation because of their ecclesiology. The role and quality of ordained leadership will be considered later, as will the comment about the lack of support for Catholic initiatives.

The important issues of finance and longer-term sustainability are also addressed. Dioceses have different policies and expectations about funding but there is a general expectation that a church plant will become financially self-supporting, including the payment of parish share within a reasonable period of time, often stated as five years. Inevitably there will be exceptions which will continue to need support, as is often the case for existing parishes. This indeed depends on the mission strategy that is being implemented and the "value" that is put on the continued existence of the plant, by the plant itself, by the sponsoring church and ultimately by the diocese. There is an unspoken assumption in many dioceses about church plants that they simply cannot be allowed to fail.

The report looks at how church plants engage with their local communities. Some engage in the sense of offering activities which are in general evangelistic. Others offer activities which fill some unmet community need. However, the picture is a continually changing one as plants look at different ways of engaging, alone or with others, with their local communities. The original vision is likely to be modified over time as a church plant should be seen as dynamic and so be able to adapt quickly to changing circumstances. This is an important factor for many church plants.

In considering the area of growth, the report agrees that this is not easy to assess, either in crude numerical terms or in levels of discipleship and commitment. Some large charismatic churches see growth in terms

---

[84]   *From Anecdote to Evidence*, p. 49.

[85]   *From Anecdote to Evidence*, p. 49.

of self-replication, i.e., when a plant grows to a certain size, it itself spawns a new plant elsewhere. On this subject, the report concludes that plants need to be sufficiently reflective both to work out what they want to become and to assess what they are actually becoming.[86] In their concluding remarks, the authors refer to the many different types of approach, stressing the need for flexibility, creativity and above all, welcome.[87]

The Victorian Anglo-Catholics

As noted above, the seeming lack of enthusiasm for mission and evangelism on the part of much of today's Anglo-Catholic constituency is in marked contrast to that of its Anglo-Catholic forebears. Pickering, in *Anglo-Catholicism: A Study in Religious Ambiguity*, devotes a whole chapter to mission.[88] He recounts the activities of many renowned Anglo-Catholic priests, e.g., Fr Walter Hook, Fr Charles Lowder, Fr Mackonochie, Fr Dolling, Fr Benson with his founding of the Cowley Fathers and Fr Stanton. Their exploits have also been well documented in other studies.[89] However, I will be looking in Chapter 4 in detail at the work of two lesser-known Anglo-Catholics, whose lives are only recorded in biographies, long out of print, but it is important to introduce them briefly at this point as they provide a link with church planting activity in the past. They each exemplify in different ways the spirit of Anglo-Catholic mission and church planting/building in the Victorian era.

---

[86]   *From Anecdote to Evidence*, p. 68.

[87]   *From Anecdote to Evidence*, p. 70.

[88]   W. S. F. Pickering, *Anglo-Catholicism: A Study in Religious Ambiguity* (London: Routledge, 1989). Reference is to paperback version (London: SPCK, 1991), pp. 65–87.

[89]   E.g., Geoffrey Rowell, *The Vision Glorious* (Oxford: Oxford University Press, 1983; paperback: Clarendon, 1991), George Herring, *What was the Oxford Movement?* (London: Continuum, 2002), John Shelton Reed, *Glorious Battle* (Nashville, TN: Vanderbilt University Press, 1996).

The first is a priest, Fr Richard Temple West (1827–93), who was responsible for the building of St Mary Magdalene, Paddington. The information plaque on the nearby canal towpath states: "The parish was founded in 1865 as a *church plant* (my italics) from All Saints, Margaret Street in a densely packed slum district by Fr Richard Temple West."[90]

His biography, verging on a hagiography, was written by the renowned Anglo-Catholic priest, Fr T. T. Carter of Clewer, who was an older contemporary.[91] There is also a collection of service registers from St Mary Magdalene, held at the London Metropolitan Archive, which show something of the activity and finances of the church, although as far as celebrating the Eucharist was concerned, West left much of this to his colleagues, except for festivals and a regular Thursday service. What his biography does cover is the range of activities designed to respond to the social and educational deprivation that West found through his parish work and the finance that was raised to support these as well as other causes both outside of the parish and abroad.

The second person is Richard Foster (1822–1910), a banker and merchant of the City of London, mentioned briefly above in connection with Walthamstow.[92] His biographer was his son, William, so the biography is written from a much more personal perspective than that of West. He also has the advantage of the intimate knowledge from his involvement in what appears to be a close-knit family. In addition, because of Foster's position in the City, he was a member of a number of committees and charities, and their records concur with what is in his biography. Foster provides significant evidence of the role that philanthropy played in the building of new churches in the Victorian era.[93] As many of his donations

---

[90] This plaque introduced me to Temple West who was previously unknown to me.

[91] T. T. Carter, *Richard Temple West—A Record of Life and Work* (London: J. Masters & Co., 1895).

[92] W. F. Foster, *Richard Foster* (London: Eyre & Spottiswood Ltd., 1914. For private circulation).

[93] For a very full account of Victorian philanthropy see Sarah Flew, *Philanthropy and the Funding of the Church of England 1856–1914* (London: Pickering & Chatto, 2015).

were given anonymously, it is only from his biography that we can have some indication of the scale and range of these donations, the information having been derived from the records that were meticulously kept by his secretary and confidante, Mr Townsend (the biography does not refer to him by any other name).

Conclusion

In this chapter, I have sought to engage with theological and ecclesiological issues for Anglo-Catholics around the Fresh Expressions agenda and especially around church planting. I have shown some of the aspects around church planting towards which Anglo-Catholics might have negative views. They see that there is the lack of a clear ecclesiology. Again, although *MSC* affirms the need for the dominical sacraments as a mark of being an Anglican church, it acknowledges difficulties in putting sacramental worship into practice, especially as so many Fresh Expressions are lay led. Anglo-Catholics could see this as a significant barrier to engagement. Thirdly, the lack of an obvious continuity with what has gone before in the life of the Church would raise serious concerns for Anglo-Catholics.

I have described the history and context of the Fresh Expressions and church planting initiatives which have become an important feature of the way in which the Church of England sees mission in the twenty-first century. I have related some of the criticisms and objections raised by several Anglo-Catholic theologians whilst also challenging a number of the assumptions that lie behind these. I have also drawn attention to the most recent literature which deals specifically with church planting in an Anglo-Catholic context. In addition, I have pointed to the activity of church planting of two Victorians who had a vision for mission and the role of new churches and who, in their differing ways, put this vision into practice for the extension of the Kingdom of God. These areas will be further expanded in the later chapters of this book as three current church plants are described based on participant observation and brought into conversation with the activities of Richard Temple West and Richard Foster.

2

The context of Victorian Anglo-Catholicism

A definition of terms

This chapter aims to give a historical context in which to set the work of Richard Temple West and Richard Foster in the second half of the nineteenth century. Their lives and work will be discussed in the following chapter. Although the phrase "Anglo-Catholicism" is used both in my title and in this chapter, in the nineteenth century and subsequently, various different terms, including "Anglo-Catholic" and "Tractarian", were in use and their meanings were often confused, overlapping and not clearly defined. For the sake of clarity and consistency, I will use the term "Anglo-Catholic" whilst recognizing that it might be regarded in some contexts as anachronistic.

The particular tenets of Anglo-Catholicism can be described in two ways. First, there was an acceptance of the general formulation by the late fourth-century monk, Vincent of Lérins: *"quod semper, quod ubique, quod ab omnibus creditum est"*.[1] This continued to be one of the touchstones of Anglo-Catholic belief. However, it is obviously open to dispute as beyond the creeds, particularly the Nicene Creed, the status and existence of other beliefs and practices were much more in doubt.[2]

---

[1]   "What is to be believed, is what has always been believed, everywhere, and by all." W. S. F. Pickering, *Anglo-Catholicism: A Study in Religious Ambiguity* (London: Routledge, 1989), p. 156.

[2]   This was the creed defined at the Council of Nicaea in AD 325, refined at the Council of Chalcedon in AD 451 and used in the service of Holy Communion.

Secondly there is Pusey's much more specific definition which clearly encapsulated the beliefs of those who would later come to be called Anglo-Catholics and which would still be generally accepted today in most Anglo-Catholic parishes, whether liberal or traditional.[3] This has previously been described in detail. It can be seen therefore that the thrust of the Anglo-Catholic position was a resort to antiquity and a link to the apostolic and post-apostolic church as recorded by the early Church Fathers. Pickering regards this concept as "static and backward looking" and as a result, out of keeping with the needs of the present-day church.[4]

Introduction and historical background

The late eighteenth-century Church of England is often portrayed as a quiescent church, comfortably existing in what was believed to be the God-given social structure of the squire and the parson, in which every member of the parish knew their place. This was especially true in the countryside where most people still lived. This superficial and often accepted view is not necessarily an accurate description of the significant variations in the practices across the Church during the Hanoverian Period, as Mather contests.[5] His article about the Georgian church gives examples of widespread disparities. Later, Mather documents the range of worship activity in parish churches, using archdiaconal visitation records. He shows that many churches held two Sunday services (double duty), a long one in the morning, consisting of Morning Prayer, Litany, Ante-Communion and Sermon, and a shorter one of Evening Prayer

---

[3]   It will be seen later that there were also a number of liturgical acts that could be added as identifiers of Anglo-Catholic practice and were seriously challenged in the latter half of the nineteenth century as a result of The Public Worship Regulation Act 1874.

[4]   Pickering, *Anglo-Catholicism*, p. 156.

[5]   F. Mather, "Georgian Churchmanship Reconsidered: Some Variations in Anglican Public Worship 1714–1830", *Journal of Ecclesiastical History* 36:2 (April 1985), p. 265.

in the afternoon, usually, but not everywhere, without a sermon. The infrequency of the celebration of Holy Communion was one of the factors that the Oxford Movement wanted to address. Again, Mather shows that the picture was not a monochrome one; rather there were significant variations across England and Wales.[6] The general themes of Mather's arguments are accepted by Walsh *et al.* In their introduction, they refer to the "great residual vitality of High Churchmanship" during this period.[7] Further in the same chapter, they refer similarly to the growing strength of Evangelicalism.[8]

There were, however, significant social distinctions in parish churches. Rented box pews were the norm in most churches for those parishioners who could afford them. The rented pew system provided a steady source of income for a church and those who opposed its abolition did so as much for financial reasons as for any social motives. Pew rents paid for the upkeep of the church building and subsidised the ministry. If they were abolished, how would the financial shortfall be made up? Against this, the later Anglo-Catholics looked to the offertory and tithing as the proper way of funding parishes; but this was still a contentious issue.[9] At the same time, the Church and the State were seen as a unity, and it was the role of the Crown to uphold this arrangement, as through Parliament it ordered the affairs of the Church.[10] Indeed, even as late as 1848, Cecil F. Alexander, the wife of William Alexander, the future Anglo-Catholic Archbishop of Armagh, would write:

---

6   Mather, "Georgian Churchmanship Reconsidered", p. 269ff.

7   John Walsh, Colin Haydon and Stephen Taylor (eds), *The Church of England, c.1689—c.1833: from Toleration to Tractarianism* (Cambridge: Cambridge University Press, 1993), p. 32.

8   Walsh et al., *The Church of England, c.1689—c.1833*, p. 49.

9   As an aside it is worth noting that in the contemporary Church of England, most Evangelicals would support tithing and direct giving, but other parts of the church still very much rely on "fundraising activities".

10 Geoffrey Rowell, *The Vision Glorious* (Oxford: Clarendon Press, 1991), p. 1.

> The rich man in his castle, The poor man at his gate,
> He made them high and lowly, And ordered their estate.[11]

The *status quo* was seemingly fixed in the early Victorian Church.

However, in the first part of the nineteenth century, this social view and the demography of the nature of the Church had already been significantly challenged. The repeal in 1828 of the Test and Corporation Acts, the Catholic Emancipation Act 1829, and then the 1832 Reform Act meant there was now the situation in which Parliament, with Dissenters and others, could legislate for the Church of England. As a result Parliament was seen by many churchmen to be tainted by the inclusion of non-Anglicans and so unfit for the purpose of the governance of the Church. Additionally, what many believed to be innocent and sensible proposals were put forward by the then Whig government to reduce the number of Irish dioceses.[12] This caused among others a great upsurge of antagonism and claims of Erastianism, a sign of the control of the State over the Church.[13]

At the same time, there were also serious concerns in the University of Oxford that the dilution of Anglican identity as was being seen in Parliament could also happen in the University following the admission of Dissenters and Roman Catholics both as undergraduates and to College Fellowships. The Universities of Oxford and Cambridge at that time were still the main training ground for the clergy and most unmarried college

---

[11]   A verse of the hymn "All things bright and beautiful" now expunged from modern editions of hymn books.

[12]   The Church of Ireland, the Established Church, in effect a branch of the Church of England, was very much in the minority in a "country" in which Roman Catholicism was the predominant denomination in the South and Presbyterianism the dominant force in the North. Hence it was sensible and logical to reduce the number of bishoprics. This today is reflected in the diocesan titles of many current Irish bishops such as the Bishop of Kilmore, Elphin and Ardagh, which includes the names of these abolished bishoprics.

[13]   The Shorter Oxford English Dictionary defines this as "the theory of the supremacy of the State in ecclesiastical affairs".

fellows were ordained.[14] They saw the Anglican identity of the university as *sine qua non*.

Sociologically things were also changing. The industrial revolution was bringing people into towns for work and the parish structure and church provision were becoming inadequate for the growing population. Whatever else the Reformation had accomplished in theological terms, it had not changed the medieval parochial structure of the Church of England which was still heavily biased towards rural parishes. The ancient endowments of the Church were not linked to any form of pastoral need and advowsons (the right of a patron to present a clergyman to a living) were openly traded. In contrast, in the growing urban areas, many churches had insufficient income to support a priest and so the pastoral needs of parishioners could not be met.[15] There are some resonances here with the way in which current Anglo-Catholic plants are supported financially.

Those clergy in the late eighteenth and early nineteenth centuries who held a "high" view of the Church also linked this with a high view of the State and hence the role of the Crown in Parliament. The High Church ideal of the late eighteenth century was "of a practical and orthodox faith rooted in the Church of England's doctrines and sacraments".[16] During the premiership of Lord Liverpool (1812–27), several High Churchmen were promoted to the episcopal bench and the group known as the "Hackney Phalanx" prospered.[17]

---

[14] University College, Durham had been founded in 1832 by Bishop Van Mildert with the Dean and Chapter of the Cathedral. King's College, London was founded in 1829 by King George IV and the 1st Duke of Wellington, but it was a number of years before their graduates were acceptable for ordination.

[15] Pastoral needs cover what now are generally referred to as "Occasional Offices" as well as parish visiting which was seen to be a key area of a parish priest's work outside of the duty to provide worship.

[16] Rowan Strong (ed.), *The Oxford History of Anglicanism, Volume III: Partisan Anglicanism and its Global Expansion 1829–c.1914* (Oxford: Oxford University Press, 2017), p. 144.

[17] Strong (ed.), *The Oxford History of Anglicanism, Volume III*, pp. 144–5.

However, their influence diminished after the resignation of Liverpool who was succeeded briefly by George Canning and then by the Duke of Wellington, under whose premiership the Corporation Act was repealed in 1828 allowing Nonconformists to hold office in public life. The Roman Catholic Emancipation Act passed in 1829 gave similar rights to Roman Catholics. This appalled high churchmen generally as a betrayal of the constitution and their fears were further raised when a Whig government was elected in 1830 with Earl Grey as Prime Minister. On this government's agenda was "Reform" of government in general as well as its relationship to the Church. This caused concerns in the minds of many with the possibility of disestablishment and the severance of the relationship between Church and State as had happened in the 1790s in France.

The Assize Sermon and *Tracts for our Times*

The perceived danger facing the Church of England was expressed most clearly by the Oxford poet and priest, John Keble, in his Oxford University Assize Sermon of 14 July 1833, which he entitled "National Apostasy". He identified that the current trends in political life were alienating society from the Church and thereby were damaging the spiritual life of the nation. To counter this Keble and others developed a strategy which involved writing tracts under the general title *Tracts for our Times*, seeking to address the important issues facing the Church at that time. The final tract, *Tract XC*, written by John Henry Newman of Oriel College and Vicar of the University Church of St Mary the Virgin, was the most controversial. It was entitled *Remarks on Certain Passages in the Thirty-Nine Articles*. Its aim was to show that the Book of Common Prayer and the Church of England had a Catholic rather than a Protestant identity. It was on this basis that what we now call Anglo-Catholicism developed.

Reactions to *Tract XC* and the Crisis of 1845[18]

The period following the publication of *Tract XC* continued to be one of controversy. Newman struggled to convince both his supporters and antagonists as to his *bona fides* as a loyal and orthodox Anglican. Newman's opponents were not slow in circulating copies of the Tract to the Heads of Colleges within the University as well as to some bishops. What most damaged Newman was Bishop Bagot's charge at a clergy assembly in Newman's church and in his presence.[19] This statement was in direct contradiction to Newman's view that the Articles had been written in a deliberately ambiguous way in order to gain wider acceptance. Furthermore, it led to a wider range of episcopal condemnation and Newman began to realize that his views were becoming increasingly unacceptable across the Church of England. His reaction was to resign as Vicar of St Mary's in September 1843 and to withdraw to Littlemore, a hamlet south-east of Oxford where, in 1836, he had established the Church of St Mary and St Nicholas as a daughter church of St Mary's. Newman resigned his fellowship of Oriel College on 3 October 1845 and was received into the Roman Catholic Church on 9 October 1845.

The years following 1845

After Newman's conversion to Rome, the role of standard bearers for the Anglo-Catholics fell to Pusey, Keble and Charles Marriott, the Dean of Oriel College. Newman's conversion, and that of others, gave the lie to the claim that Anglican Orders were shared on an equal footing with the other two "branches" of "The One Holy Catholic and Apostolic Church"

---

[18]   This period has been documented in depth in chapters by Michael J. G. Pahls and Kenneth L. Parker as well as by Sheridan Gilley in Stewart J. Brown, Peter Nockles and James Pereiro (eds), *The Oxford Handbook of the Oxford Movement* (Oxford: Oxford University Press, 2017). This chapter sketches an outline in order to put the work of West and Foster into their historical context.

[19]   Richard Bagot was Bishop of Oxford from 1829–45 and hence the bishop to whom Newman owed "canonical obedience" as defined in his institution oaths.

(as the Nicene Creed has it), the Church of Rome and the Orthodox Churches of the East.

However, Pusey had other interests which took precedence over the departure of Newman. He had, anonymously, endowed the building of St Saviour's Church in Leeds, with the acquiescence of Walter Hook, the Rector of Leeds. Pusey's view of Newman's departure was summed up in a very charitable and forgiving statement:

> [Newman] seems then to me not so much gone from us, as transplanted into another part of the Vineyard, where the full energies of his powerful mind can be employed, which here they were not.[20]

Keble was looking for a safe way out of the dilemma. He found comfort in Bishop Butler's words a century previously that the "safer way" is always to be preferred even in the teeth of seemingly contrary evidence.[21] The next challenge that arose, almost as an unexpected but probably inevitable consequence, was ritualism with which Anglo-Catholics became aligned.

Ritualism

One of the central tenets of Anglo-Catholicism is that the public worship of the Church should mirror its theology and ecclesiology, and this should be seen to be worthy of the message of the gospel. This view also coincided with the growing interest in medievalism, antiquarianism and romanticism in England generally and especially among many younger clergy. Matins and Evensong were the normal forms of worship and Holy Communion was celebrated in most parishes on a monthly or less frequent basis with few communicants, as frequent communion

---

was uncommon among laypeople.[22] Richard Foster in the middle of the nineteenth century wrote in a letter:

> To me it seems absurd to suppose that persons with little or no education and without religious convictions or feelings will ever be drawn into our churches, or kept when there, by the perpetual monotonous reading of 'When the wicked man . . .' and 'Dearly Beloved . . .'

This statement, from a very devout Anglican who attended church most days for Matins, demonstrates the gap between churchgoers and the population at large. Geoffrey Rowell quotes a similar view from an essay by the Revd James Edward Vaux written in 1868:

> Without laying ourselves open to the charge of a morbid craving after unhealthy excitement, we may venture the opinion that the repetition of 'Dearly Beloved Brethren' at the least seven hundred and thirty times each year, is calculated to become a little wearisome by the time we have reached mid-life.[23]

Although Ritualism has been linked with the Oxford Movement, its origins go back much further. Bishop William Van Mildert, Bishop of Durham from 1826–36, as far back as 1797 commented:

> Some of the most admired parts of our Book of Common Prayer are taken almost literally from the Romish Ritual: and this, far from being any just objection to it, proves that the compilers were guided by the genuine spirit of moderation and Christian candour.[24]

---

[22]   F. Mather, "Georgian Churchmanship Reconsidered", p. 272.

[23]   Geoffrey Rowell, *The Vision Glorious* (Oxford: Clarendon Press, 1991), pp. 121–2.

[24]   Quoted in Peter B. Nockles, *The Oxford Movement in Context: Anglican High Churchmanship 1760–1857* (Cambridge: Cambridge University Press, 1994), p. 219.

The drive for more solemnity and seriousness in worship, reflected in a more defined ritual, was also influenced by two antiquarian societies that were in the most part dominated by clergy, the Cambridge Camden Society and the Oxford Society for Promoting the Study of Gothic Architecture.[25] There was a growing belief in many quarters that the worship of God demanded the highest quality of response that human beings could give, and in the minds of a growing number of clergy, that implied a more structured ritual. In many cases, initially that meant no more than a strict adherence to the rubrics of the Book of Common Prayer.[26] Yates comments that Keble was one of the most cautious of the Tractarian leaders who never moved far from the High Churchmanship in which he had been brought up.[27]

However, after Newman's defection in 1845, the move for a more elaborate form of ritual grew. A strong view now arose that the church building was set apart, sacred for the worship of God. Thus, worship should be more in keeping with the apostle Paul's command, "that all things should be done decently and in order" (1 Corinthians 14:40). Pews were moved to face the altar, which was given prominence.[28] As a result the large three-decker pulpits which had often dominated the nave were sidelined. More regular services were established and clergy began to dress in more appropriate robes, e.g., cassock and surplice, although for many years there was still a backlash against wearing a surplice for preaching instead of the traditional black gown.[29] This ritualistic movement grew and is relevant to the churches which I will describe in Chapter 5 as two of them use Anglo-Catholic ritual which is identifiable with what "the ritualists" were propounding.

---

[25]   Nigel Yates, *Anglican Ritualism in Victorian Britain, 1830–1910* (Oxford: Clarendon Press, 1999), p. 219.

[26]   Pickering, *Anglo-Catholicism*, p. 19.

[27]   Yates, *Anglican Ritualism in Victorian Britain*, p. 55.

[28]   William Bullock (1797–1874) wrote a hymn which contains these words: "We love thine altar, Lord, Oh what on earth so dear". This was subsequently revised by Sir Henry Baker (1821–77).

[29]   In the mid-1960s, I visited a "black gown" church in Manchester, and the father of the late Bishop Stephen Sykes was also in that tradition.

What then emerged as the great area of contention was the "Ornaments Rubric" in the Preface to the 1662 Book of Common Prayer. It stated, quoting Section XIII of the Act of Uniformity 1559, the first year of the reign of Queen Elizabeth I:

> Provided always, and be it enacted, that such ornaments of the church, and of the ministers thereof, shall be retained and be in use, as was in the Church of England, by authority of Parliament, in the second year of the reign of King Edward VI, until other order shall be therein taken by the authority of the queen's majesty, with the advice of her commissioners appointed and authorized, under the great seal of England, for causes ecclesiastical, or of the metropolitan of this realm.[30]

This posed two problems, one obvious and the other more arcane. The first was how to identify what ornaments had been in use nearly 300 years previously, with very little documentary evidence; therefore, of what did "ornaments" comprise? Were they fixtures like statues, or did they include vestments or even what was done in the liturgy? There was no agreement on this. The evidence was scarce and there was an over-reliance on funerary ornaments in churches which often were a matter of artistic interpretation rather than a liturgical statement.[31] Secondly there was no agreement of the exact dating of the "second year of the reign of King Edward VI". The way of calculating this was a matter of dispute and so could not be agreed. Hence there was recourse to the earlier and less "reformed" editions of the Prayer Book (e.g., the 1549 version), its rubrics and injunctions. These issues caused confusion and dissension but equally provided an opportunity for some to take advantage of this ambiguity to establish their own positions.

Over the next decades those early Anglo-Catholics attempted to introduce a number of practices into their regular worship which they

---

[30] Section XIII of the Act of Uniformity 1559. <https://history.hanover.edu/texts/engref/er80.html>, accessed 18 January 2023.

[31] Sculptors would usually portray their subjects in the best and most imposing way, even if the vestments they portrayed had never been worn by the subject.

claimed, under the terms of the Ornaments Rubric, to be legal, but were contested by their opponents. These are generally agreed to be:

- the use of Eucharistic vestments such as the chasuble, alb, maniple and stole;
- the use of a thurible and incense;
- the use of "lights" (especially the practice of putting six candles on the high altar) when light was not required for reading;
- the use of unleavened (wafer) bread in communion;
- eastward-facing celebration of the Eucharist (when the priest celebrates facing the altar from the same side as the people, i.e., the priest faces east with the people, instead of standing at the "north side" of the "table" in the chancel or as required by the rubric in the 1662 Book of Common Prayer);[32]
- the mixing of sacramental wine with water.

For mission-minded Anglo-Catholics, the aim was to ensure that those who engaged with their worship should experience something numinous, something of "the other", however that might be conceived. The intention was, as Pickering states, that congregations should be made aware that they were worshipping in the House of God, a building set apart and held to be sacred.[33] This was particularly true in the poorer parts of towns and cities where many Anglo-Catholic priests worked. Peter Doll writes:

> R. F. Littledale in 1868 pointed out that London gin palaces were complete with "internal decorations, abundant polished metal and vivid colour, with plenty of bright lights". Why should the church not use the same means? "Ritualism is a sort of excursion

---

[32] There has always been confusion about what this means. The historical view is that the Holy Table was at that time placed lengthwise in the chancel and the people gathered opposite the priest who therefore was on the north side. In those few churches which still aim to follow this rubric, it seems that the minister (they would not use the word priest) officiates from the narrow north end of an eastward-located "table".

[33] Pickering, *Anglo-Catholicism*, p. 20.

train on Sunday, to bring the poor man out of his dull, squalid, every-day life into a land of beauty, colour, light and song".[34]

The natural concomitant to the highly decorated building was an elaborate and matching ritual but one that should not be ritual for ritual's sake. Ritual was to be seen as the action that must express doctrine. Pickering comments that ritual is worthless unless based upon sound doctrine.[35] Ritual should have a far more important role than just making churches pretty, colourful or less boring—although by default, it had accrued this role to itself in the eyes of many who attended. The controversy over ritualism continued over the second half of the nineteenth century and into the twentieth. Evelyn Underhill quotes from W. H. Frere's *The Principles of Religious Ceremonial*:

> No one can hope to judge fairly of matters of ceremonial who does not see that the reason why they cause such heat of controversy is that they signify so much.[36]

But by the middle of the twentieth century many of these practices had become part of the normal style of worship in much of the Church of England.[37]

---

[34]   Stewart J. Brown, Peter Nockles, and James Pereiro (eds), *The Oxford Handbook of the Oxford Movement*, p. 368. The original of the quotation from Littledale which Doll cites is to be found in John Shelton Reed, *Glorious Battle: The Cultural Politics of Victorian Anglo-Catholicism* (Nashville, TN: Nashville University Press, 1996), p. 150.

[35]   Pickering, *Anglo-Catholicism*, p. 21.

[36]   Evelyn Underhill, *Worship* (London: Nisbet & Co. Ltd., 1936), pp. 23–4.

[37]   A significant number of clergy currently would normally be wearing some form of vestments, at least an alb and stole; candles were *de rigeur*, although six was a marker of a "high church"; wafers were usual in the majority of Anglican churches, as much for convenience as for any theological reason; the eastward-facing position had been adopted until after Vatican II when most Anglo-Catholic clergy followed the Roman change and adopted the westward-facing position with altars moved into the body of the church.

This section has outlined the context in which I can proceed to describe the life and work of Richard Temple West and of Richard Foster.[38] The information is derived from their extant biographies. It is acknowledged that biographies are clearly open to bias, both positive and negative. That of West is almost a hagiography, whereas Foster's has the bias of being written by a son about a greatly loved and respected father. However, both the contemporary records of the *Church Times*, the *Evening Standard* and other organs, and original material currently held in archives, either physically or in a digital format, corroborate the statements in the biographies.

Today only traditional Anglo-Catholics as a norm take the eastward-facing position. Others may do so on specific occasions.

[38]   T. T. Carter, *Richard Temple West—A Record of Life and Work* (London: J. Masters & Co., 1895). W. F. Foster, *Richard Foster* (London: Eyre & Spottiswood Ltd., 1914) (private circulation). Both of these biographies, long out of print, are accessible in the British Library and the Cambridge University Library.

3

Two Victorian church planters

The Reverend Richard Temple West

In his introduction to his biography of Richard Temple West, T. T. Carter states that he was not intending to describe a life but rather to portray the "attractive and influential personality of one who seemed to keep with true consistency a high religious aim".[1] He locates this in the context of the difficulties faced by clergy who had enthusiastically embraced the Oxford Movement. He further quotes the Bishop of Nassau, a friend and supporter of West, as saying that West encouraged "a spirit of hopefulness" which was part of the mission of the Church of England.

Early life and education

West was born on 29 April 1827 to John West, a barrister who was also a Commissioner in Bankruptcy, and Lady Maria West, daughter of the Earl of Orford and also distantly related to the Earl of Delaware, so, in UK terms, one of the nobility. He was sent to Eton College in 1839 and went as an Exhibitioner to Christ Church, Oxford in 1845. He was known for his devoutness, but he was also a keen sportsman. Christ Church was not involved in the Oxford Movement, which had its academic base at Oriel College. In contrast, it had arranged for its compulsory church services to take place at the same time as those of churches which were supporting the Oxford Movement in order to prevent its students and fellows attending and being influenced by the teachings of Newman and his followers.

---

[1]   T. T. Carter, *Richard Temple West—A Record of Life and Work* (London: J. Masters & Co., 1895), p. iii.

On graduating, West moved to London where he became a pupil barrister at Lincoln's Inn from 1850–3. He was much in demand at society events as a skilful dancer, but his religious devotion was obvious as he started visiting the poor. This religious devotion was the spur which took him away from the law to prepare for ordination.

The start of ordained ministry

West went to Cuddesdon Theological College for his training, which had recently been established by Samuel Wilberforce, Bishop of Oxford, and he was subsequently ordained. His initial curacy was at Leeds, where the rector of the parish church was Walter Hook, a formidable high churchman. It would seem that West's curacy was not a happy one as he only stayed in Leeds for a year. Although Carter skates over the reasons for his departure, it can be surmised that Hook and West had a difficult relationship as West was a stickler for the rigid adherence to the Prayer Book rubrics whereas Hook wanted to ensure that his services were accessible and so "bent the rules" to make this happen. Richard Foster's view about Hook's services is referred to later in this chapter.

In 1854, West moved to St Mary's, Hemel Hempstead as curate. *De facto* he was in charge of the parish, as the vicar, Henry Mountain, was very frail and usually not well enough to lead worship. Mountain did not want any changes made to the style of worship, but West caused an outrage when he inserted the Prayer for the Church Militant before the Blessing in the Ante-Communion Service.[2] He caused further upset when he provided bookmarks, embroidered with crosses, for use in the service books. Another cause of dissension was his invitation to Edward Monro to preach at the opening of the new school building. Monro was Vicar of Harrow Weald and a noted preacher and writer but was a firm supporter of the Tractarians. There were demonstrations which Carter regards as being on the same level as those at St Barnabas, Pimlico and

---

[2]   It needs to be noted that in this period with the growth of the influence of the Oxford Movement, any changes to the Prayer Book liturgy, however small, were met with deep suspicion.

St George-in-the-East some years previously.[3] West was burnt in effigy, alongside that of the pope, at the Guy Fawkes Day commemorations in 1856.[4] These "innovations" were in themselves fairly trivial, but they introduced an element of change which was unacceptable to the conservative views of the worshippers who could not condone this. This factor is as important in the reaction to the introduction of any apparent Anglo-Catholic practice as any doctrinal argument against such practices. From many years of personal experience, I can confirm that many church congregations are very conservative and unwelcoming of change.

However, the crisis which ended West's curacy in 1857 was a result of his intransigence in respect of what many would now consider to be a matter of secondary importance. Queen Victoria had given birth to a daughter, Beatrice, on 14 April 1857. The Privy Council issued a Prayer of Thanksgiving for the Queen's safe delivery of the baby and commanded it to be read in churches. West objected, as it had been issued by a secular authority and not by the bishop. George Murray, Bishop of Rochester, believed it already had been lawfully issued and therefore did not consider it necessary to issue it in his name. He was unable to persuade West to accept its authority as West had declared that he would not use the prayer unless it were personally authorized by Murray. In a letter published in the *Morning Post* on 18 August 1857, West set out his version of events. His main contention was that in his oath of canonical obedience, he had sworn only to use those forms of service laid down in the Book of Common Prayer. In addition, as he was not the vicar, only an assistant curate, he had no authority to change anything and as

---

3   These are both well-documented examples of the resistance to the introduction of Anglo-Catholic practices. See George Herring, *The Oxford Movement in Practice* (Oxford: Oxford University Press, 2016), p. 174.

4   The Prayer Book at that time contained an order of service entitled "A FORM of PRAYER with THANKSGIVING to be used yearly upon the Fifth Day of *November;* For the happy Deliverance of King JAMES 1, and the Three Estates of E N G L A N D, from the most traitorous and bloody-intended Massacre by Gunpowder: And also for the happy Arrival of His Majesty King WILLIAM on this Day, for the Deliverance of our Church and Nation", which was discontinued in 1859 (capitals as in original text).

noted above, Mountain did not want changes made. Stalemate ensued and Murray felt that in face of such disobedience, he had no option but to inhibit West's ministry.

In spite of these difficulties, West's three years at Hemel Hempstead had many positive aspects. He was known in the parish as an assiduous visitor and energetically sought children for baptism. One Sunday he baptized 35 children and the following week another 12. He was responsible for the rebuilding of the church school, as well as the removal of the box pews from inside the church. As a parting gift to the parish, he had the Norman west door restored. He was fondly remembered by many in the parish for the faithfulness of his ministry despite the difficulties there had been, which for most of his congregation were irrelevant.

West next moved to be curate to William Gresley who was rector of the newly built church of All Saints, Boyne Hill, on the outskirts of Maidenhead. The church, designed by George Street, had been paid for by three wealthy women to provide a church for Anglo-Catholic worship. Gresley had in 1851 written *The Ordinance of Confession* which had caused great controversy. Many in the Oxford Movement were encouraging individual confession to a priest as a laudable spiritual practice which had a rightful place in the Church of England. However, this was condemned as popery by Evangelicals and others.[5] It was this alleged use of confession that led to West's departure from Boyne Hill.

The circumstances are as follows: on one occasion he had visited a seriously ill woman who had led a very dissolute and profligate life.[6] Using the Prayer Book Office of the Visitation of the Sick, he encouraged her to confess her sins openly and receive absolution in the form prescribed.[7] A neighbouring incumbent complained to Bishop Wilberforce that

---

[5]   W. S. F. Pickering, *Anglo-Catholicism: A Study in Religious Ambiguity* (London: Routledge, 1989), pp. 77–84.

[6]   Carter, *Temple West*, p. 28.

[7]   The Rubric states: "Here shall the sick person be moved to make a special Confession of his [sic] sins if he feels his conscience troubled with any weighty matter."

West had forced this woman to make a personal confession.[8] Bishop Wilberforce was reluctant to act against West but, under pressure from *The Times* (which at that time was taking a close interest in church affairs, especially when there seemed to be a challenge to the Protestant nature of the Church of England), he eventually set up a commission to hear the accusations against West. It is worth noting that, on hearing of this, Walter Hook of Leeds asked to appear "to give evidence against Mr West". This perhaps sheds some light on the reason that West's curacy in Leeds only lasted for a year. The hearing lasted for 11 hours at the end of which West was cleared of the charge of forcing a confession. However, West felt unable any longer to remain at Boyne Hill as he was sure his opponents would always be looking to find reasons to make further complaints against him.

W. J. E. Bennett had previously been forced to leave St Barnabas, Pimlico, as a result of his extreme ritualistic practices and subsequent demonstrations against them; he became Vicar of St John the Baptist, Frome in Somerset in 1852 which he established as a significant centre of Anglo-Catholic worship. West was invited to work with him on a temporary basis. He was very popular, and Bennett asked him to stay at Frome to take charge of the Choir School. Much as West might have been tempted, another opportunity was offered to him, which was to prove to be the most significant part of his ministry.

Ministry in London—The establishment of St Mary Magdalene, Paddington

The Margaret Street Chapel had existed near Oxford Street since the mid-eighteenth century. It had more recently become influenced by the Tractarian Movement and in the 1840s Frederick Oakeley, the vicar, conceived a plan to have it replaced with a building more fitting to Tractarian worship. Oakeley became a Roman Catholic in 1845, following the example of Newman. His curate, Upton Richards, then became vicar. Richards continued to support Oakeley's plan for the replacement of the chapel with a church more in keeping with the Tractarian style of

---

8   This type of complaint was quite common between the different factions in the Church at this time.

worship. He was strongly encouraged in this by the Cambridge Camden Society which strongly believed that Gothic architecture was the most appropriate vehicle for the fitting worship of God. The old chapel closed on Easter Monday 1850 and the foundation stone of the new church, designed by William Butterfield, was laid by Edward Bouverie Pusey on All Saints' Day (1 November) the same year. The building took over eight years to be completed but was consecrated on 28 May 1859. It was to this church that West came as curate in 1860. As was his pattern, he was conscientious in his ministry, especially in visiting the sick and the poor. The seeming arrogance which had caused him problems both at Hemel Hempstead and at Boyne Hill appeared to have been ameliorated. Booth notes that All Saints did not have a parish of any size, but the poor were helped by it as well as by two other fashionable parishes, the firmly Evangelical All Souls, Langham Place and the high church St Andrew's, Wells Street. Because of its reputation for supporting the poor, it was even suggested that the rents in the poor streets around All Saints were affected.[9]

After a few years, some of the residents of Paddington, who worshipped at All Saints, came up with the idea of founding a mission in the Paddington area with a similar style of worship to that of All Saints to avoid the necessity of a tedious journey to Margaret Street.[10] West, with the enthusiastic support of Upton Richards, was asked to look at ways in which to realize this vision. Every Saturday he went to Paddington to look for a site on which he might build a church. He eventually found one, a cramped sloping site between the Paddington arm of the Grand Junction Canal and a crowded slum area. A modern information board on the towpath of the canal describes St Mary Magdalene as "a church plant from All Saints, Margaret Street". This was a significant impetus for my research.

The immediate area around the church consisted of housing for poor people. Booth, around 50 years later, described it as "a most unsatisfactory

[9] Charles Booth, *Life and Labour of the People in London, Third Series: Religious Influences*, Volume 2 (London: Macmillan & Co. Ltd., 1902), p. 199.

[10] This was both a convenience and also a mission opportunity to a very deprived and depraved area.

spot".[11] He goes on to relate that houses are let on a daily basis, often to different tenants by day and by night, and that thieves and prostitutes formed much of the population. Obviously, the area had declined since the church was first built as Booth says: "This district is an example of what has gone wrong."[12]

West was renowned as a skilled collector of charitable funds and soon he had sufficient funding to start work and a temporary "tin tabernacle" dedicated to St Ambrose was opened in February 1865. He started with six services on Sundays and soon instituted a daily celebration of the Eucharist. The *Church Times Supplement* of 7 April 1866 describes the Three Hours' Agony service on Good Friday: "The people were most devout—indeed throughout Lent, as *John Bull* observes, the congregation in this church have [sic] been, perhaps, the most remarkable in the diocese of London."

The life of the Church of St Mary Magdalene

West's skilled fundraising enabled work to begin on the church building, designed by George Street, and when it was decided to enlarge the original plan, to extend the church building rather than incorporating a clergy house, two ladies sold their house, furniture and jewellery which just met the additional cost of the extension as well as paying for some of the ornaments and fittings, and donated this to West. The altar was carried from the temporary church and the Eucharist was first celebrated in the still incomplete church on 21 October 1868. The *Evening Standard* the following day described this event: "The church was crammed; hundreds of people were standing and many others were turned away. The service was conducted in accordance with the principles of the advanced High Church School."[13] All was due to be finished by St Mary Magdalene's Day (22 July) 1872.

Unfortunately, whilst the roof was being completed, a workman set fire to the roofing felt. It quickly took hold and the roof crashed into the nave, causing significant damage. The altar and other furnishings

---

[11]   Booth, *Life and Labour,* Volume 3, p. 121.

[12]   Booth, *Life and Labour,* Volume 3 p. 124.

[13]   *Evening Standard,* 22 October 1868. Accessed via British Newspaper Archive.

were saved and removed to St Ambrose's Chapel where ten services were held the following day, the first at 4 a.m.[14] Rebuilding began straight away, and West at St Mary Magdalene's set a standard for devout and sincere worship. Pews were all free and the sexes sat separately, which a chronicler thought "a wise precaution that ought to be adopted in all places of worship".[15] Another journal records that on Easter Sunday 1872 there were six celebrations of the Eucharist, no fewer than 1,122 communicants and an offertory of £1,180.[16] This shows the significant influence that West had in encouraging support for the work of the church. Unfortunately, there is no breakdown in the Services Register to show how these amounts were made up.[17] St Mary's was not unique in this respect as on Easter Day 1876 at St Augustine's, Kilburn, the offertory amounted to £1,343 with 621 communicants.[18] Thirty years later the *Daily News* census of 1902–3 recorded a Sunday attendance at St Mary's of 863: 152 men, 646 women and 65 children. However, the census only recorded attendances at one morning and one evening service.[19] It would therefore appear that the attendance at St Mary's was holding up 30 years after its opening and nearly ten years after the death of Richard West.

West's ministry was not confined to worship. The educational and social needs of his parishioners also occupied his mind, as there was little other publicly provided provision at that time. During West's ministry, St Mary Magdalene's gained responsibility for a Choir School, a Sisters' Home, a Penitentiary Home, a Working Men's Club, a Nurses' Institute, private schools for different classes and a daughter church, St Martha's, which offered a simpler style of worship. The Bishop of Nassau, a friend and supporter of West who had been a priest in London prior to his consecration, commented that it was one of the most notable home

14   Carter, *Temple West*, p. 36.

15   Carter, *Temple West*, p. 39.

16   This is over £105,000 at the time of writing according to the Bank of England inflation calculator.

17   The Service Registers are held at the London Metropolitan Archive.

18   *Church Times*, 21 April 1876.

19   Richard Mudie-Smith (ed.), *The Religious Life of London* (London: Hodder & Stoughton, 1904), p. 101.

missionary efforts in any English parish.[20] The work was augmented by two establishments in other parishes, a facility where female prisoners could complete their prison sentences and a Sanatorium for Inebriates. All of these activities were under West's care and support.[21] He also aimed to undertake five hours' visiting a day. Booth in 1902 notes other areas of social support like a thrift organization, sick clubs and a goose club. He says:

> In such ways the church makes itself felt, and also through its schools. In the day school there are no less than 1200 children, including many of the roughest.[22]

West's conduct of worship was reverent and devout. He took it seriously and was intolerant of any sloppiness or casualness in the vestry or during the service. His curates were impressed by this as were "outsiders" who attended St Mary Magdalene. His pastoral care, both towards his parishioners and towards the many others with whom he communicated by letter, was assiduous. This extended even to animals. Carter records that on one occasion West saw a horse struggling to pull an overloaded cart up a hill. He immediately went to push the cart and encouraged bystanders to join him in this effort.[23]

During the mid-1860s, there was a move for Parliament to reform parts of the Prayer Book. West vigorously opposed this, as he did with any other attempt to influence or regulate the conduct of worship by a secular authority as he believed it to be wrong. He financially supported clergy who were being prosecuted for their ritualistic practices, although he had not by any means adopted these himself. He only began wearing vestments when others were being prosecuted for doing so. He regarded such legislative interference as unconstitutional. In 1871, he, with other clergy, wrote to John Jackson, the Bishop of London, protesting against a judgement of the Judicial Committee of the Privy Council which

---

[20]   He also contributed a chapter to Carter's biography.

[21]   Carter, *Temple West*, p. 44.

[22]   Booth, *Life and Labour,* Vol. 3, p. 123.

[23]   Carter, *Temple West*, p. 61.

admonished the Revd John Purchas for performing certain ritualistic liturgical acts. The bishop's reply to West, supporting the judgement, was published in full in the *Church Times*.[24]

Two other aspects of West's ministry need to be considered, both of which can be said to be relevant to modern church planting. First was his devotion to the work of the Sunday School. He would try to call in every Sunday to greet the children who attended, and they saw this as a high point of the day. They would be upset if he failed to appear.[25] He always joined the Sunday School summer treat to the fields around Harrow. In the early years, the children travelled by barge, but when the numbers became too great and hence dangerous, the journey was made by train. West joined in the games for as long as his health allowed, but he always aimed to take part in some way. Many church plants today (as well as other more traditional churches) place great emphasis on working with children as a way of gaining an opening into the wider community of adults. The Fresh Expressions concept of Messy Church relies on this by involving parents in the craft and other practical activities arranged for children.

The other important aspect was his involvement with the wider church. West took a prominent role both in the work of the Society for the Propagation of the Gospel in Foreign Parts, and the Society for the Promotion of Christian Knowledge. He saw his involvement in these as a way of countering the influence of the Evangelical wing over the missionary activity of the Church of England. From 1882, he was also on the Governing Council of Keble College, Oxford which had been founded in 1870. This shows a breadth of vision which should be an exemplar for those involved in church planting. A plant/new church does not exist *in vacuo*; it is an integral manifestation of the Body of Christ and so should relate to other parts of that Body for mutual support and influence. It is sad that, anecdotally, many current church plants avoid involvement in the wider structures of their dioceses and so become *de facto* congregationalist.

---

[24] *Church Times*, 26 May 1871, p. 233.

[25] Carter, *Temple West*, p. 65.

The final years

All of this activity eventually had an effect on West's health. For the last ten years of his life, he would spend part of the winter in Cannes as chaplain, to counter the winter weather and air pollution in London which was causing him severe chest problems.[26] He was forced to reduce his workload because of repeated bouts of uncontrollable coughing. He had typhoid fever in the winters of 1887 and 1888. His visits to Cannes led him to say, "all coughing and sneezing gone".[27] He seemed to recover some of his strength in 1891 but by May 1892, his health was further declining. Christmas Day 1892 was the last time he was in St Mary Magdalene's. He was too weak to celebrate the Eucharist but did administer the chalice. He attended Evensong and received the Offertory and gave the Blessing. During this time and until his death, he was cared for by one of the Sisters of Mercy from their community at Clewer. He received communion for the last time on 2 February, when the Reserved Sacrament was brought to him from the church. He also wanted to see his sister in Bournemouth, and although he was very weak, his doctor thought it would be of benefit to him to be away from London. On 9 February, he was taken by ambulance to Waterloo Station and went by train to Bournemouth. However, the journey proved too much for his weakened body, and he died the following morning in Bournemouth at 2 a.m. The next day his body was transported to Waterloo where it was met by his clergy colleagues. The dining room of his vicarage in Delamere Terrace was converted into a chapel of rest where his body remained until it was taken into church on 13 February where a vigil was kept. His funeral took place the following day followed by a Requiem High Mass. He was buried in Willesden Churchyard. He had begun his work at St Mary's on 14 February 1865 and was buried on that same day 28 years later.

---

26   Having independent means, he could support this, although on several occasions he was supported by the Prince of Wales.

27   Carter, *Temple West*, p. 91.

Conclusion

West was a truly remarkable priest. In his obituary in *The Times*, he was referred to as "one of the most prominent and respected High Church clergy of the metropolis".[28] The *Church Times* also carried a very long obituary, as did other publications; as an example, *The Indicator* of 17 February 1893 carried a very effusive tribute as well as an extensive description of his funeral.[29] His energy for his parish work and his care for his parishioners and all who came to him for spiritual support were exemplary. The social and educational work which he established at a time and in an area where few such resources were provided shows a man who put the social implications of the gospel into practical effect. By doing this, he foreshadowed the words of Bishop Weston to the Anglo-Catholic Congress of 1923:

> Go out and look for Jesus in the ragged, in the naked, in the oppressed and sweated, in those who have lost hope, in those who are struggling to make good. Look for Jesus.[30]

His legacy continues today. St Mary Magdalene's is still open for worship. Although it had fallen into some disrepair, it is now being restored for the worship of God and as a place to support the wider community and the arts.

Richard Foster, a merchant of London and philanthropist

Richard Foster's biography was written by his son William. He wrote:

---

[28] *The Times*, 11 February 1893, p. 10.

[29] *The Indicator*, 17 February 1893, p. 168.

[30] Geoffrey Rowell, *The Vision Glorious* (Oxford: Clarendon Press, 1991), p. 242.

It seemed right, to us, his children, that the life and work of Richard Foster should be written for the encouragement and benefit of his descendants.[31]

William had the benefit of access to the very detailed notes and diaries that his father had compiled over the years and the biography contains copious verbatim quotes.

Foster's background and early life

Foster's family came from Stainforth, near Settle in North Yorkshire, where they had lived for many generations. His grandfather was a blacksmith and ran a smallholding, but although the family had once been prosperous, by the time of his great-grandfather Thomas, "the family had fallen on bad times".[32] So Thomas, the eldest son, was sent to London, where his uncle, a clergyman, lived. His brother John later joined him as did the other brother William (Foster's grandfather). William gained employment in the Bank of England. The brothers prospered in business, as commission merchants (importers) trading with Portugal and Brazil.[33] This was the family background into which Foster was born on 4 September 1822 in Finsbury. His father was 47 years old and his mother 37. He was an only child, and his parents had thought that they would never have children. He was baptized on 11 October 1822. His schooling was of a private nature and at one stage he boarded with a clergyman.

When he was 13 and a half, Foster's father decided that he should make arrangements for his future; he gave him two options: he could study for Holy Orders or go into his uncles' business. As he had a strong disliking for Latin and Greek, which was an essential component of training for ordination, he stated that he would prefer to work in the office. Although called a clerk, he was more of an office boy as his uncles

---

[31]   W. F. Foster, *Richard Foster* (London: Eyre & Spottiswood Ltd., 1914), Preface—no page number.

[32]   Foster, *Richard Foster*, p. 7.

[33]   Like many families in the eighteenth and nineteenth centuries, sons were given the same names as their fathers, so confusion is very possible.

believed that he should start at the bottom, doing mundane tasks such as cleaning. Foster's father died in 1837. Foster remained as a clerk until 1852 when he became a partner in the business with his cousin. He continued to live with his mother even after his marriage in 1858, until he bought a house on Clapton Common in 1862.

Foster's reaction to the state of the Church

Richard Foster was very devout and would attend Morning Prayer at West Hackney Parish Church each day and then walk to his office in Moorgate. This devotion to worship was one of the drivers of his life. William notes that the time in which his father lived was one of great change in society with a growing emphasis on the need for reform. The Church was no exception to this. William Foster wrote about the state of the Church:

> The bulk of the clergy had become apathetic and dull, performing with an easy-going acquiescence the perfunctory discharge of formal duties. The church as it had been in the eighteenth century was scarcely adapted to the needs of more stirring times.[34]

Into this context came the Oxford Movement which "deeply affected my father, and from it his work received its inspiration".[35] Besides the emphasis on regular worship and the sacraments, William Foster emphasized Dean Church's view that the Oxford Movement led also both to an increased study of the Gospels and to more self-discipline. As a result, it became very clear to many that the structures of the Church no longer met the missional and pastoral needs of the nation.

Richard Foster had been taking an interest in church extension since before 1848. He regularly attended West Hackney Parish Church and was concerned that there were not enough "free seats for the poor".[36] (This

---

34 Foster, *Richard Foster*, p. 40. For an alternative view, see F. Mather, "Georgian Churchmanship Reconsidered: Some Variations in Anglican Public Worship 1714–1830", *Journal of Ecclesiastical History* 36:2 (April 1985), pp. 255–83.

35 Foster, *Richard Foster*, p. 42.

36 Ibid., p. 44.

was before the abolition of box pews and pew rents.) He is recorded as being disappointed that he "did not succeed in stirring up the West Hackney people to take up the subject of Church extension".[37] He earlier had been so concerned about the lack of mission activity that he donated the £2 that his mother had given him (from her very limited resources) on his twenty-first birthday, anonymously, to the National Society. This set him on the course which he was to follow for the rest of his life.

Foster's philanthropy

Much of the financial support in the middle of the nineteenth century that the Church of England received both for its ongoing worship and the maintenance of its buildings came through philanthropy.[38] The first new church in which Foster was involved was that of St Matthias, Stoke Newington. Together with Dr Richard Brett and others, he held a public meeting on 16 October 1848 to consider whether a new church was needed to minister to this area. The decision was in the affirmative. The church school was built and used for worship just over a year later. The erection of the church followed, and it was consecrated on 13 June 1853. Foster wrote in considerable detail about this project, as he also did about his last project, the building of St Barnabas, Walthamstow in 1902. His view on philanthropy can be seen as follows:

> From the year 1858 my Book, which I call my Charitable Gifts Book, gives an account of the chief amounts of what I have given away under the name of Charity.[39]

This book records that between 1858 and his death in 1910, he gave away about £380,000—a sum documented in his biography—sometimes in small but often repeated amounts. It contains nearly 10,000 entries.

---

[37] He wanted to build two side aisles to increase the capacity of the church.

[38] For a comprehensive and well-researched account of this, see Sarah Flew, *Philanthropy and the Funding of the Church of England, 1856–1914* (London: Pickering & Chatto, 2015).

[39] Flew, *Philanthropy and the Funding of the Church of England, 1856–1914*, p. 53.

He was also open to appeals for support but objected as a matter of principle to bazaars and raffles as ways of funding church building. To such requests he would send a pamphlet that he had written giving his reasons.[40] His secretary, Mr Townsend, kept the record and oversaw the distribution of the donations which covered a wide range of recipients. The main ones were either individual building funds or centrally organized schemes such as the Bishop of St Albans' Fund which was to support churches in the eastern part of London, which at that time were in that diocese. In 1872, he set aside £100,000 for charitable giving, but gave away far more. He seemed on occasions almost to be embarrassed by his business success. He ensured that funds were paid through the right channels, because as a businessman he saw that "finance is a matter over which the average clergyman is not infrequently a sad bungler".[41] A complete record of his donations no longer exists but numerous reports in the *Evening Standard* over the period of his lifetime refer to donations to and involvement with both the repair of churches and the building of new ones. I cite six examples:

- 19 May 1873, Foster is referred to as "a munificent contributor" to St Faith's, Stoke Newington. The *Church Times* of 28 March 1872 when reporting the laying of the foundation stone on 25 March 1872 describes his "known liberality in Church building".
- 30 December 1874, Foster laid the foundation stone of St Peter's Vicarage, Hoxton Square as he had been a generous benefactor to the District.
- 29 October 1875, the Bishop of Rochester used Foster as an example of "wealthy generosity".
- 30 January 1879, Foster chaired a meeting to look at the spiritual needs of Hackney Wick. He offered £100 towards the £1,000

---

[40] Unfortunately, in spite of the assistance of extensive research by a number of supportive librarians and archivists, I have been unable to trace an extant copy of this leaflet. At that time, Anglo-Catholics were promoting the offertory and tithing as the way of funding the Church, whereas Evangelicals were holding fundraising events such as bazaars and whist drives.

[41] Foster, *Richard Foster*, p. 81.

needed to purchase a site for a church and additionally offered to add £5 to every £100 collected.

- 20 October 1881, Foster offered to pay for the repairs to the outside of the decaying church of St Mary, Haggerston, provided that the parishioners would cover the cost of the interior refurbishments.
- 26 November 1906, in an article about a visit by the Bishop of London to St Michael's, Shoreditch, Foster is described as "a rich London merchant who contributes to a group of churches in the area".

Foster's views on worship

The way in which the normal worship of the Church was seen to be boring seriously concerned him. His view was confirmed and his outlook enlightened when he attended a service conducted by Walter Hook in Leeds Parish Church:[42]

> [This] taught him also that there could be no fixed rule as to what type of service was right, and that in different times and in different congregations a different degree of ritual might be desirable.[43]

He wrote at length about how Morning and Evening Prayer, with their repetition of seemingly incomprehensible scriptural sentences and the recitation of "Dearly beloved brethren", were alien to the masses and almost in an unknown language.[44] He wanted something to stir the imagination—energetic sermons that would be relevant to the thoughts and feelings of the poor. Churches should contain what is stirring and beautiful as a witness to the honour due to God. He concluded a letter on this subject by writing:

---

[42]   This was the same Walter Hook to whom Richard Temple West had been curate some ten years earlier.

[43]   Foster, *Richard Foster*, p. 61.

[44]   The introductions to Morning and Evening Prayer in the Book of Common Prayer.

The highest form of worship on earth should be a reflection of that which is rendered in heaven, and the great end of all the subordinate ministries of the church should be to prepare souls to this end in their measure and degree.[45]

It was to those churches that were providing worship in line with this view, or that as new churches would follow this example, that he gave his support.

Merchant of London, supporter of church building and of the clergy

Foster firmly believed that as his money had been made in and through the City of London, it should be used to support London (in its broadest definition). He was particularly concerned about the growing area of Walthamstow. It had been a small Essex village with a population of 3,006 in 1801 and just over a century later had become an urban part of London with a population in excess of 120,000.[46] In 1840, there was one Anglican church, the historic parish church of St Mary; by 1911 there were 18. Of these Foster, with his cousin John Knowles, paid entirely for the construction of St Saviour's Church in 1874. He also contributed to the funding of the building of other churches in Walthamstow. His uncle James had lived there, and, in his legacy, had asked Richard Foster to "remember Walthamstow". This he did and his passion for church building is seen in a pamphlet that he wrote in 1881 entitled *Some Wants of the Church at Home and Abroad; With Suggestions How to Supply Them*:

A great and terrible fact meets our eyes at every turn, and it is this, that, in all our dense centres of population, by far the greatest portion of our people are as yet unreached by the working

---

45   Foster, *Richard Foster*, p. 64.

46   Steven Saxby, *Anglican Church Building in Victorian Walthamstow* (London: Walthamstow Historical Society, 2014), p. 3.

machinery of the Church, and for want of it, are, in too many cases, living a life of utter ungodliness.[47]

This is echoed by George Haw in Mudie-Smith's *The Religious Life of London* written at the beginning of the twentieth century. He laments the fact that what were previously rural hamlets, and he included both Walthamstow and Tottenham in this category, have become replicas of the East End. He records a former council chairman as saying:

> Tottenham ... has practically become another Bethnal Green. Formerly it was a middle-class residential place, but almost all the good houses have been removed to make way for working-class dwellings. The place fell a prey to the jerry-builder when cheap railway fares were introduced, and the evils then committed have never been remedied.[48]

For Haw all the negative aspects of East End life were now replicated in places like Walthamstow and Tottenham. Foster was involved in the building of St Michael's, Walthamstow, but his *pièce de resistance* was the Church of St Barnabas. He had already purchased a site and had erected a "tin tabernacle" in 1899 but intended later to provide a permanent building.[49] He laid the foundation stone for this building in 1902, and on it were inscribed these words, carved by Eric Gill:

> This church of St. Barnabas Walthamstow is to be built at the cost of Richard Foster a merchant of London as a thanksgiving to Almighty God for numberless mercies during a long life. This

---

[47]   Ibid., p.10 quoted from p. 2 of Richard Foster, *Some Wants of the Church At Home and Abroad; With Suggestions How to Supply Them* (London: Rivingtons, 1881). This pamphlet was reviewed in the *Church Times* of 4 February 1881.

[48]   Mudie-Smith (ed.), *Religious Life*, p. 341.

[49]   This is still in use by a secular organization. Saxby, *Anglican Church Building in Victorian Walthamstow*, p. 20.

stone was laid by the aforesaid Richard Foster on 4th September 1902, being the day on which he completed his 80th year.

The building was completed and consecrated on 7 November 1903.

In 1862, Foster had moved from his family house in Stoke Newington to a house on Clapton Common; his mother also moved. By 1879 he was finding London too polluted and crowded, so he bought a house in Chislehurst, called Homewood, where he lived until his death. The house in Clapton was loaned to the London Diocese to house the newly appointed Suffragan Bishop of Bedford, William Walsham How, who had responsibility for churches in north-east London. Foster had also offered £12,000 towards the stipend costs of Bishop How. This offer was never taken up as the vacant living of St Andrew Undershaft was given to the bishop, and its endowment was more than sufficient to support his ministry.

The move to Chislehurst did not lessen his support for the north London churches, and he was involved in a plan to establish five district parishes in Tottenham. In addition, as he travelled by train each morning into the City, he also saw the crowded districts in south London with few churches. He therefore became a firm supporter in 1883 of the plan by the Bishop of Rochester to build ten new churches and he offered funding for two clergy for two years in two Mission Districts in the hope that these districts would eventually become new parishes. He also was keen on the idea of "associated parishes", that is, the linking of a rich parish to support a poor parish both in workers and finance. Thus, he supported the linking of the parish of Chislehurst, where he was now worshipping, with the deprived parish of St Katherine's, Rotherhithe and hoped other wealthy parishes would follow that example.[50]

But Foster was not only concerned with church building and expansion. He was a founding member of the Candidates Ordination Fund, which aimed to support young men who had little financial backing of their own, to train for ordination. He saw this as important as widening access to the ordained ministry. He also actively promoted and supported, as one of the founder members, the Sustentation Fund

---

[50]   *Church Times*, 7 March 1884, p. 175.

for Parochial Clergy (later renamed the Queen Victoria Clergy Fund) which sought to raise all stipends to £300 a year. He said that:

> ... the time had now come when we must think of the incomes of the Clergy. It is no use building Churches and having no Clergy to minister in them.... The living voice would make itself heard, but the building without the voice would not.[51]

The condition of the clergy continued to cause him significant anxiety until his death. His oft-repeated phrase was, "Living voice rather than buildings of brick and stone."[52]

Foster was also involved in more secular charitable work, such as the London School Board. He was treasurer of the London Hospital and established a convalescent home in Brighton. He was involved in a number of housing improvement schemes and introduced co-partnership into the South Metropolitan Gas Company in which he was a large shareholder. An acquaintance, the Revd W. T. Brown, wrote of Foster: "His life was in every way ideal. I have never known anyone who loved to do good as he did."[53]

As he grew older, he reduced his visits to the City office to once a week, although a desk was always made available for him. He spent more time at home, but also often visited his married children, and he celebrated his golden wedding in 1908 at Romsey Abbey where he had been married, in the company of all his children and their families.

By the summer of 1910, Foster realized that his health was failing, and he began to make arrangements for his death. He sorted out the cheques he expected to send at Christmas to parishes and other beneficiaries and said farewell to his children. His favourite daily prayer at that time was the *Te Deum*. He died surrounded by his family on 23 December 1910. His body was taken into Chislehurst Church on 27 December, and he was buried in Chislehurst churchyard. The *Te Deum*, his favourite devotion, was sung instead of a closing hymn at his funeral. The Bishop

---

[51]   Saxby, *Anglican Church Building in Victorian Walthamstow*, pp. 129–30.

[52]   Saxby, *Anglican Church Building in Victorian Walthamstow*, p. 130.

[53]   Saxby, *Anglican Church Building in Victorian Walthamstow*, p. 138.

of St Albans later paid tribute to him as "one of the heirlooms of the church".[54] He saw the needs of the Church and used his wealth to meet some of them. But he was a visionary; he saw beyond bricks and stone to the needs of those to whom the Church seemed irrelevant. He wanted to plant a Christian presence where there was none; so, the presence of a priest was in the immediate term more important than the existence of a church building. He was pleased to use his influence as well as his wealth as a way of ensuring that this would happen. Although describing himself as a "Prayer-Book Churchman", he could clearly see that there was need of other ways in which the Church should engage with the growing population with a more accessible form of worship. Above all, he saw that faith needed to be put into practice rather than being imprisoned in buildings, important as these might be.

West and Foster as Victorian examples of church planting

When one considers the lives of these two men, who in differing ways worked towards the outreach of the mission of the Church of England into areas where it seemed to be absent, one is struck by the similarities of character and approach. West was a priest, and Foster was proud to be a lay merchant.

When West's ministry in Paddington is considered, there is an overwhelming sense of intentionality and of being driven. West's earlier altercations with episcopal authority had given him the ability, where necessary, to tread lightly on the "rules" if he saw them as an impediment to his ministry. His establishment of St Mary Magdalene was driven by his vision for that place. Nothing, not even a devastating fire, would stop him from setting up this church with a large functioning building. He was so successful that he was eventually embraced by "The Establishment", as his obituary in *The Times* bore witness.[55] This parish had become his life's work and his relational, pastoral and missional engagement with a

---

54   Saxby, *Anglican Church Building in Victorian Walthamstow*, p. 155.

55   *The Times*, 11 February 1893, p. 10.

very different social class is evidence of this. He was a man with a clear vision of what he wanted to achieve. This was for him essential in his planning for a new church. He was not willing to accept any obstacles so that when the fire occurred, he immediately continued his work as if nothing had happened. He wanted this church to succeed, and he did everything to ensure its success, even to the extent of sacrificing his health through overwork.

In the same way, Foster was driven. After the first setback at West Hackney, where his plan for expanding the church building was rejected, he ensured that his money would be used for extending the witness of the Church. The way in which he organized his philanthropy made certain that it was not wasted. His giving was focussed on specific projects in which he had the confidence that his financial contribution would be well used, and the projects would be successful. He became engaged in the different organizations that were supporting the physical growth of the Church in London but also was not afraid to challenge them. His moral and financial support for a new bishopric to support the work of the Church in east London is testimony to this.[56] His commitment from his early years to the expansion of the witness of the Church is key to how he made sure that his giving would be appropriately used for the mission of the Church in that historical period.

West and Foster, in very different ways, had a clearly focussed vision for the growth of the Church in Victorian England. Whilst doctrinal and ecclesiological arguments were raging and threatened to tear the Church of England apart, their commitment to the preaching of the gospel and the Church's witness to it made all of these arguments irrelevant. They both provide striking examples of how the work and the witness of the Church can continue on a local level in spite of more widespread controversy and dissension. Both West and Foster saw a church building with its priest, located in a community, as the focus for Christian ministry and mission, although as has been noted earlier, Foster placed a higher priority on the priest. It is also true that in Foster's case, new parishes

---

[56]   The suffragan see of Bedford was revived in 1879 in the Diocese of London after being supressed since 1560. As noted above, Foster offered his house in Clapton for the bishop to live in.

were also created around the churches whose building he had supported. The vision of both men was to ensure that the Church was openly present among the people to witness through Word and Sacrament to the saving love of God in Jesus Christ and to serve them as he would desire.[57] This also is the vision behind modern Anglo-Catholic church planting.

---

[57]   Mark 10:45.

4

Three modern church plants

Introduction

The origins of the three churches which I selected for my research, and so are described in this chapter, are very different and this was one of the reasons for their selection. They are situated in parishes with an above average level of deprivation; in fact all of them are located within the bottom twenty-fifth percentile of parishes in England in the official deprivation index that the Church of England uses to rank parishes. This was not a deliberate part of the research design but provides a useful counter to the "urban myth" that church plants work best in middle-class areas and attract young middle-class worshippers.[1] In this chapter, I will describe these three churches on the basis of their monthly attendances over a period of 18 months. This should enable the reader to engage with me in describing the life of these churches. I believe that from this regular and consistent in-depth involvement in the Sunday life of these churches, important lessons and themes can be identified which will have implications for those clergy and others who might be considering similar developments. I have anonymized the churches and the clergy involved, but as far as possible, the descriptions of each church will follow the same structure to allow some sort of comparability. Statistical information is given for each parish as a whole.[2]

---

[1]   The two books by Tim Thorlby cited in the bibliography also debunk this myth.

[2]   I need to add a caveat to this statement. In the case of St Paul's, Melchester, the church is a plant in a very large existing parish, Christ Church, so statistical information exists for the parish as a whole, rather than for the immediate

Each section will begin with recounting an incident which seems to me to say something important about the church and its setting. I will then provide statistical data around population, deprivation index, ethnicity and religious affiliation for the area in which the plant is located.[3] I will complement that with a physical description of the church building, its surroundings and the parish as a whole. The next section will give the background to the establishing of the plant. I will then proceed to describe a typical service both in terms of liturgical style and also the make-up of the congregation and other factors that I believe to be significant. I will conclude with any issues that may not have been covered in the above framework. The purpose of these descriptions will be to show the variety of worship and other aspects of church and community life in church plants founded across the spectrum of current Anglo-Catholicism as well as to bring them to life. These descriptions and my later analysis are designed to provide evidence that Anglo-Catholic church planting is an acceptable way in which churches can meet the needs of their communities and wider groups of worshippers and so engage (and be seen to be engaging) in mission. They can also provide "lived examples" for others to emulate.

The purpose of this type of description is to link the real-life experiences of participant observation research with a later theological analysis. John Van Maanen, an American academic who has written widely on ethnographical research methods, uses the phrase "impressionistic tales"

---

area served by the plant. It is difficult to assess if the area served by the plant is very different demographically to the parish as a whole. A similar problem but with less significance arises in respect of Holy Cross, Greystone, in that it is situated in the parish of St Clement's; however, this is a much smaller parish in area and is very much more uniform in its types of housing so there should not be significant differences.

3   The statistics in this chapter are taken from the 2018 Diocesan figures based on the most recent published data from the Office of National Statistics. The deprivation index runs from 1—the most deprived—to 12,500—the least deprived.

to describe such a process.[4] This helps to remove some of the element of subjectivity from the account and also helps locate the description in place and time and show that "lived reality". This also shows that clergy and others in ministerial roles engage with the real lives of their congregations rather than using an abstract theological theory.

St Pancras, Rushey Common

The morning of Sunday, 23 September 2018 dawned grey and very wet with a large amount of surface water on the roads. Trains and tubes were inevitably delayed, and when I reached the bus stop outside Rushey Common tube station, I saw that the bus, which stopped right outside the church, was late as well. My regular practice had been to get to church early so that I could see the congregation gathering. This was not going to happen today. A bus did come, and I arrived at church at 9.58 a.m. I went in and saw just two people, the churchwarden Susan and Fr Francis, the vicar. Others slowly came in ones and twos. However, by ten past ten, after we had struggled through the opening hymn, "Lord God, your love has called us here", there were 25 adults, ten children and a dog. (This animal was brought most weeks by his owner and generally sat quietly on the pew beside her, except when it joined in to share the Peace.) This unpunctuality of those who attended, although not usually as extreme as on this particular Sunday, was typical, as it was of the two other churches in this study. I have considered what this means both specifically in regard to St Pancras and also more widely for these three churches. I was brought up to be in church well before the start of the service. I conclude that it is one indication of the more informal nature of twenty-first century society, just as many people now attend church services dressed in a much more casual way from previous generations who would always wear their "Sunday best".

---

4   John Van Maanen, *Tales of the Field: On Writing Ethnography* (Chicago, IL: University of Chicago Press, 2011), p. 4.

Background to the plant and its development

St Pancras was built in 1915 and was part of a large benefice. There was the parish church, St Martha's, and another church, St Augustine's. There is also another parish with a church in the centre of Rushey Common, St John's. This arrangement lasted for many years, but by the second decade of the twenty-first century it became obvious to the diocesan authorities that it was no longer fit for purpose and the churches were seen to be "failing". A report from the Area Bishop in 2014 about future plans put it thus:

> However, times and demographics move on, and we have to organize the church for our contemporary missional challenges and not stick with structures that have served us well in the past but may not be fit for purpose in the present.[5]

In 2014, with the retirement of the Vicar of St Martha's and the move to another post of the Vicar of St John's, there occurred the opportunity for "pastoral reorganization".[6] The bishop felt that this was an opportunity not to be missed. St Martha's was to be joined to St John's and with it, part of the parish of Rushey Common. St Augustine's had ceased having regular services and after being used for a short time by another Anglican congregation, had been made redundant. The Diocesan Board of Finance had tried to sell it for housing but was unsuccessful. It was therefore decided to detach it from the parish of Rushey Common and reopen it, linked to a nearby thriving Evangelical church, St Matthias. This left St Pancras. The plan was to ask a nearby well-attended and active Anglo-Catholic church (St Paul's) to take responsibility for it as a "graft",[7] but obviously the agreement of that church was needed as it would have resource implications, both human and financial. The alternative was

---

[5]   From an internal diocesan document supplied to me by the Area Bishop.

[6]   Pastoral reorganization in the Church of England can involve rearranging parish boundaries, merging separate parishes into a combined benefice and even closing churches.

[7]   This is the preferred term in the Diocese of London for linking a "failing" church with a thriving church to attempt to bring it back to life.

that St Pancras would be closed. The purpose of the graft was set forth as follows:

- To renew St Pancras in worship and mission;
- To enable a refreshment of the congregation with some new blood from St Paul's;
- To help St Pancras focus on outward-facing mission;
- To improve footfall in a building that is "hidden" to many parishioners.[8]

This was agreed, with the Vicar of St Paul's writing:

> Further to our meeting, and your letter of the 20th June 2014, our PCC [Parochial Church Council] has met to discuss the proposal. I am delighted to say it received an extremely positive response and we are very interested in exploring the proposal even more. The PCC wish me to say what an interesting and exciting prospect this is for us a church which we believe will have wider congregational support too.[9]

Obviously, this could not be achieved overnight. The vicar and a newly arrived associate priest, Fr Francis, spent time sharing their vision for St Pancras. They described the vision in these terms:

> We wish to re-evangelize Rushey Common by building a strong sense of community and a solid worshiping and engaging congregation within the Anglo Catholic tradition and serving the Local Community through social transformation.

They wanted St Pancras to be:

---

[8]   From an internal diocesan document sent to the PCC of St Paul's and supplied to me by the Area Bishop.

[9]   From the document referred to above.

> A place for those seeking meaning and purpose in their lives and where walking through the door would mean getting into a world of caring, and a deepening of their spiritual lives where nobody feels excluded and all can be open to experience the love of God in Jesus Christ.

They envisioned the church building to be a "place where locals can meet, a place for art, music, dance, social and cultural events, a place for meeting neighbours and other members of the community".[10] This is now happening with the church being used for mindfulness classes as well as musical and theatrical events in addition to the regular worship; the acoustics of the building are particularly suited to such activities. The most important factor was to "keep the doors open" to show that the church was "in business". Very early on in the life of the graft, a barn dance was arranged to take place in the church hall. At the last minute, it was decided to use the main church, as it provided a larger space. This made a powerful statement about how the church wanted to be seen.

A very robust strategy was devised to ensure the implementation of these proposals. Together with the associate priest, a number of parishioners committed themselves to moving from St Paul's to St Pancras towards the end of 2015 to reinforce the small congregation. Some of these people still worship at St Pancras, whilst others have either moved away from the area or returned to St Paul's. In legal terms, the Vicar of St Paul's is the Vicar of St Pancras, but in reality the associate priest who acts as vicar has built up a solid core group of worshippers, some of whom have taken on the lay leadership of the congregation as churchwardens and PCC members.

Attendance, as in many churches these days, is an issue. As others have argued, the time when most members of a congregation attended church every Sunday has passed.[11] My experience at St Pancras was that

---

[10]   From PowerPoint presentation provided by the Vicar of St Pancras.

[11]   Trying to date the beginning of this phenomenon is very difficult and varies from denomination to denomination and even between churches of the same denomination. Callum Brown in *The Death of Christian Britain*, 2nd edn (Abingdon: Routledge, 2009), p. 1 refers to 1963 as the start of a "downward

there was a very regular weekly core of about 15 people, and then others who came less frequently, to make the usual congregation of between 35 and 40. Additionally, there would be children ranging from one to ten in number and aged up to about 11 years old. That being said, the priest has a contact list of over 500 people to whom he sends regular information about what is happening at St Pancras.

Statistical material
The tables that follow provide some basic data about the parish.

St Pancras—Population and Age Profile

Deprivation	Population	Area (Sq. Miles)	Density
2412	16478	0.5	31334

% 0–4	% 5–17	% 18–29	% 30–44	% 45–64	% 65+
8.5	13.5	17.6	29.8	21.4	9

St Pancras—Ethnicity (%)

White	Asian	Black	Mixed	Other
66.8	11.1	13.1	4.7	4.3

St Pancras—Religion Profile (%)

Christian	Buddhist	Hindu	Jewish
48.8	1.1	2.0	0.6

Muslim	Sikh	Other	None
13.9	0.9	0.5	24.5

Not Stated	7.6

There are a number of things worth noting from these figures. Seventy per cent of the parish population is under the age of 45, although children only make up 22 per cent of this number. This reflects the fact that the

---

spiral" in church attendance, but attendance had been slowly seeping away for many years prior to this.

parish does have a significant number of young professionals who are relatively mobile in employment and housing terms.

White people make up two-thirds of the population, but a large number of them, both from personal observation and my discussions with Fr Francis, whose family fits this category, are "non-British white" from many different countries of the European Union and beyond. The vicar tells me that there are significant numbers of people from Spain and Italy and as someone fluent in both languages, he sees it as part of his mission to engage with them. He holds regular Italian Masses. There are also Italian-based community activities and language classes for adults and children. Citizens from Eastern European countries are well represented, and, as an example, one Sunday I was introduced to a Russian PhD student and his Macedonian partner. People from these differing ethnicities are a regular feature of the congregation; although most of them are not Anglicans, they feel comfortable with the style of worship of this church. For those of a Roman Catholic or Orthodox background, there is some kind of liturgical and structural familiarity which would not be the case in many other church plants which have adopted a more charismatic style of worship and so generally have a more informal approach.[12]

As regards religion, Christians make up less than half of the population of the parish, which is a similar proportion to that of London as a whole according to the 2011 census figures. There is the usual range of Christian churches; for example, on the bus journey from the tube station to St Pancras, one passes a Roman Catholic church, a Baptist church, another Anglican church, a Methodist church, a Kingdom Hall of the Jehovah's Witnesses, and a signpost to a Ukrainian Autocephalous Orthodox church as well as a synagogue down a side street. The Muslim community generally is to be found in a different part of the parish, away from the church building. Its presence is most obviously noticeable in the High Street, as there are some Asian shops, selling vegetables, groceries, meat

---

[12] Although not integral to this research, it is interesting to note that in all three of the research churches, there were worshippers from a Roman Catholic background. Is this significant or yet another example of twenty-first century denominational fluidity?

and clothing. There are also a few Eastern European food shops. The second highest number is of those who state that they have "No Religion". This is almost a 5 per cent higher figure than for London as a whole but in line with the figure for the whole UK population.

The church and the parish
The church was built in 1915 for worship in the Anglo-Catholic tradition. It is perhaps one of the last churches to have been built as part of the earlier Victorian expansion of church building and so predates the inter-war church building activities in the expanding suburbs. Outside it is red brick in construction, carrying on the Victorian style of many London churches and as such very typical. The interior on the other hand is quite Italianate in design with two chapels in the south aisle and a Lady Chapel to the north side of the altar which is in an apse at the east end. There is a gallery at the west end where the organ is situated and where there is also seating for a choir. There are a number of statues of saints and of Jesus around the church, in front of which are stands for votive candles. The building is light inside and does not possess stained-glass windows. It is showing signs of past neglect with paint flaking from the very high white-painted, boarded ceiling. There are also a large number of cracks evident. The entrance to the church is via a narthex which has windows on the inside. At the east end of the south aisle is a vestry which has an entrance into the side of the sanctuary. There is the need for a significant amount of renovation, including the refurbishment or replacement of the entire roof and the heating system.

Attached to the south side of the church is a much more modern hall which is used for community activities, particularly a ballet school. As such it is equipped with a barre and mirrors all along one side. This facility provides much-needed income for the church; in 2018 the ballet school provided well over 50 per cent of the church's income, as evidenced in the annual accounts submitted to the Charity Commission. The Sunday School meets in this hall during the Parish Eucharist.

St Pancras is situated in a quiet residential area along quite a narrow road which is served by a twenty-minute interval bus service which stops outside. Opposite the church is a park with football pitches and tennis courts with a hard-surfaced path on its circumference. The houses around the church are mainly terraced, probably dating from the time just after the First World War, but they are of a good size and a number of them have been subdivided as houses of multiple occupation. The parish does not have either significant retail or business premises and is therefore virtually all residential. On the north-western edge of the parish, nearer to the tube station, there is a new development of luxury apartments on a former industrial site. The location of the church on the extreme northern edge of its parish, and the fact that it can only be seen when one is close to it, is perhaps a hindrance to its witness as it cannot rely on its visibility, unlike churches with spires or high towers. Even when one comes towards it on the bus, it can only be easily seen when one is virtually opposite it. It is particularly helpful that the bus stop is called "St Pancras Church".

Worship at St Pancras

St Pancras sits in the modern Anglo-Catholic tradition. It uses the Church of England Common Worship Order One for the Eucharist, with the occasional traditional interpolations from the Roman Rite. As an example of this at the end of the service, the priest says, "The Mass is ended: go in peace", rather than the Common Worship dismissal "Go in peace to love and serve the Lord". It is comfortable with the ordination of women to all areas of ministry and a woman associate priest from St Paul's on occasions preaches and celebrates the Eucharist. It is fully involved in the deanery and diocesan structures, unlike some traditionalist Anglo-Catholic parishes which tend to distance themselves from these.

A typical service runs as follows: a bell is rung and the opening hymn is played by the organist. A server with a thurible leads the priest (celebrant) to the altar. He may be accompanied by another priest who is the preacher for the day.[13] If so, this priest will support the celebrant as deacon.[14] The celebrant censes the altar and then is censed himself by the server. After the opening prayers, the children come to the front

---

[13] I use the male pronoun here as it is what currently happens; the regular celebrant is male.

[14] Traditionally, the deacon's role is to read the gospel and prepare the altar for communion.

and one of them receives a Bible from the celebrant who offers a prayer. They then leave for their own activities in the adjoining hall with a number of adults. An Old Testament reading is followed by a psalm with congregational responses and then a reading from the New Testament. These are always read by lay people. There is a further hymn, and the celebrant (or preacher) brings the Gospel Book from the high altar into the congregation and reads the appointed Gospel. All the readings, preaching and intercessions take place at a legilium at the front of the church. Notices and any Banns of Marriage are given before the sermon. The sermon lasts on average around ten minutes, but that is very much dependent on the preacher. After the recitation of the Nicene Creed, the intercessions are led by a lay person. One of the features of St Pancras is the way in which the whole congregation moves round to share The Peace which now follows. Everyone aims to shake hands with every other person. This can take some minutes. During the next hymn, the altar is set with the communion vessels, and the bread and wine are added and then are censed by the priest, and the congregation are censed by the server. A collection is taken and presented for a blessing. The children now return from their activities. The Eucharistic Prayer takes place and then all receive communion or a blessing. Music is played or a devotional hymn is sung during communion. Many of the congregation go afterwards to one of the votive candlestands and light a candle. (This is a practice that was new to me, but it is apparently common in some Anglo-Catholic churches.) After the altar has been cleared and the post-communion prayer said, the children come forward and describe what they have been learning and show any pictures or craft that they have done to reinforce the theme. The service ends with a blessing and the clergy process out during a closing hymn. Afterwards tea and coffee are served at the rear of the church and about half the congregation usually stays. This provides an opportunity for gathering information informally as well as sharing with other people my impressions of the worship. It also gave an opportunity for people to ask me about the progress of my research. This was personally a real encouragement.

In summary, St Pancras as a church graft/plant is beginning to show that the original vision is being brought to fruit. Community and cultural pursuits are becoming a regular part of the church's programme, as are more spiritual activities designed to deepen the faith of the participants such as the Christian mindfulness courses. The brave decision of the diocese and the willing involvement of St Paul's has enabled a vibrant Christian witness to be maintained in this part of Rushey Common. From my observation and wider church experience, I see St Pancras as a church which is beginning to fulfil the vision behind the church graft. Fr Francis has renewed the mission of the church by his outreach into and contacts with the community. The original aim of refreshing the congregation with "new blood from St Paul's" has been met as some of those who originally were involved have now returned to St Paul's, feeling that they have fulfilled their commitment. The outward-looking focus has been increased, very visibly by the use of large banners on the exterior of the long north wall of the church which faces the road and overlooks a well-used bus stop and park. Footfall has increased with a wide range of worshippers from the local area. Fr Francis commented that the population of the parish is quite transient so new people are moving in on a regular basis and a number of these have said that they came to the church as it was local.

Holy Cross, Greystone

Sunday, 25 March 2018 was Palm Sunday. The tradition at Holy Cross was that this was marked with a procession from the local park, along a couple of streets to the church for the start of Mass. Just after quarter to five, I joined the vicar and curate, carrying a number of palm branches, as well as small palm crosses which were to be blessed and handed out to the congregation. As we neared the park, a "people carrier" screeched to a halt alongside and two large, tattooed men got out. One of them asked Fr Stephen, the vicar: "Can we have one of them, Guv?" Fr Stephen responded that they had not yet been blessed. The men replied that they would wait for that to be done. After the Blessing of the Palms, the men were given one each and they then sped off. The procession of about 20 people started to walk to the church, singing: not, as I had expected, one of the traditional Palm Sunday hymns, such as "All glory, laud and honour", but the children's song "We have a King who rides a donkey" followed by "Give me oil in my lamp".

The church, the parish and the background to the plant

The parish of St Clement's was founded in 1884 and was originally part of a much larger historic—and originally rural—parish. The growth of this part of London in the latter half of the nineteenth century led to a significant amount of church building. St Clement's was built in 1887 with funding from the East London Churches Fund as well as a significant contribution from a leading public school.[15] A mission hall, which now houses Holy Cross, was built in 1891 as part of the outreach to the south of the parish. There is a clergy house attached. Whether this outreach was ever effective is a moot point. Mudie-Smith, in his report on the 1902–3 census of churches, records the attendance at a service one evening taking place in this hall of 55, comprising ten men, 30 women and 15 children, in terms of adults not significantly larger than the numbers I found in my research visits. As a comparison, St Clement's recorded 885 attendances, the second highest number in the district.[16]

The parish has changed significantly over the years and particularly as a result of immigration from the late 1940s from the Caribbean.

The mission hall had ceased to be used by the church before 1939, and it would seem that the church had forgotten about it as it was used by a number of secular organizations who neither paid rent nor made

---

[15]   The involvement of public schools as well as the universities of Oxford and Cambridge was quite common at that time both in terms of church building and in encouraging mission through the establishment of settlements. Ex-public schoolboys and others from the moneyed classes would spend some time living in more deprived parishes. This is described very well in David B. McIlhiney, *A Gentleman in Every Slum* (Alison Park, PA: Pickwick Publications, 1988). As late as the mid-1960s, as an undergraduate, I spent a number of weeks working in what was then called "The Cambridge University Mission in Bermondsey" and was, for a period, its representative on the Christian Union General Committee. It has since been renamed.

[16]   Richard Mudie-Smith (ed.), *The Religious Life of London* (London: Hodder & Stoughton, 1904), p. 404.

any effort to maintain it. St Clement's had also fallen on difficult times and serious consideration was given to its closure in the 1980s. A change of clergy led to a reassessment of the work and an emphasis on growth, not "managed decline".

Early in the twenty-first century, decisions were made which resulted in the parish reclaiming the mission hall together with the settlement of unpaid rent. These funds provided sufficient money for refurbishment. It became Holy Cross Church, and half of the mission hall building is now rented to an artists' collective which provides funding for the running of the other half of the building for church use. In 2010, regular worship began at 5 p.m. both as an alternative Mass to the 10 a.m. at St Clement's, and also to ensure Christian witness from that building in the southern part of the parish. The attached house is used for a curate when one is in post; otherwise, it is let and so provides further income.

The interior of the area used for worship is quite narrow. At one end, there is a carpeted dais on which stands the altar. Behind the altar, on a shelf, is the tabernacle for Reservation of the Blessed Sacrament, with a candlestick on either side. To the north side of the altar is a cupboard, the top of which serves as a credence table. On the south side is a chair in which the celebrant sits when he is not behind the altar.[17] There is a lectern at the front of the church, which is used for readings, intercessions and preaching. There is no musical instrument—all hymns and sung parts of the service are played through a sophisticated sound system linked to an iPod on which all the relevant music has been recorded.

There are chairs, not pews, and the shape of the building means that if all the chairs were filled, some people would not be able to see the altar. There is seating in normal circumstances for about 40 worshippers, which is at the upper end of the range of usual Sunday attendance. There is a small font by the door. There are statues both of Jesus and of the Virgin Mary either side of the altar. Behind the worship room is a corridor with

---

[17] "He" is deliberately used as the parish of St Clement's, being a traditionalist parish, has passed resolutions not to have female clergy. This also applies to Holy Cross as being part of the same parish. It is also under the pastoral oversight of the Bishop of Fulham who oversees all the traditionalist parishes in the London Diocese.

a small kitchen and WCs, although after church coffee is served from a table in the church rather than from the kitchen.

Statistical data

Holy Cross is not a parish church; it is a separate centre of worship at the extreme southern end of the parish. The parish church, St Clement's, is on the extreme northern edge of the parish and the parish boundary runs along the middle of the road in front of the church. The statistical data describes the parish as a whole, not just that part of it served by Holy Cross.

Holy Cross—population and age profile

Deprivation	Population	Area (Sq. Miles)	Density
547	10330	0.5	21027

% 0–4	% 5–17	% 18–29	% 30–44	% 45–64	% 65+
8.4	18.2	25.3	22.9	17.7	7.5

Holy Cross—Ethnicity (%)

White	Asian	Black	Mixed	Other
42.5	12.6	32.1	6.6	6.3

Holy Cross—Religion Profile (%)

Christian	Buddhist	Hindu	Jewish
52.5	2.7	2.8	0.6

Muslim	Sikh	Other	None
20.1	0.3	0.2	14.5

Not Stated	7.5

There are some important things to note from these statistics. In terms of age, the population of the parish is relatively balanced either side of 30 years old. Ethnically, white people make up well under 50 per cent of the population with a very large number of BAME people, mainly of Caribbean origin. The congregations both of St Clement's and Holy

Cross reflect this, although the part of the parish in which Holy Cross is situated is more white working class in its ethnic make-up. As regards religion Christians are just in the majority. Those who claim no religion are fewer than in the population of England as a whole. In my visits both to Holy Cross and on occasions to St Clement's, there were no obvious other places of worship which I passed. The website "A Church Near You" only identifies in the surrounding area an Islamic Centre and a meeting place of "The Family of Yahweh"—an African church, founded and based in Nigeria.[18] However, as can be seen from the statistics, the parish is geographically small and mainly made up of housing. Like many areas of London, people attend places of worship which are conducive to their preferred style of worship, often at a distance from where they live.

Worship at Holy Cross
This was an area which I found initially most confusing. Although Mass starts at 5 p.m., it is preceded by Evening Prayer at 4.30 p.m. However, it is not the form of Evening Prayer to which I am accustomed both as a worshipper and as an officiant since the Roman Breviary order is used, rather than Evening Prayer from either the Book of Common Prayer or Common Worship. This caused me confusion as the Roman Calendar refers to Sundays as the *Nth* Sunday of the Year, rather than using seasonal names, such as the *Nth Sunday after Trinity,* as the Anglican church usually does. For my early visits, I found it hard to identify which Sunday of the year it was. The short service starts with a hymn from the original edition of the *English Hymnal* followed by psalms, recited responsorially, and other short scripture readings. There is then a short time of intercession before the office finishes. There is then between ten and 15 minutes before Mass. However, during Lent, the Rosary is prayed and on Trinity Sunday there was the Office of Benediction of the Blessed Sacrament. I was not at all familiar with the Rosary, although Benediction is something I am used to.

The Mass follows the latest version of the Roman Rite in its entirety. The order is roughly similar to Common Worship, but there are variations. The significant difference is that the forms of common

---

[18] <https://www.achurchnearyou.com/>, accessed 20 January 2023.

liturgical texts, the Gloria in Excelsis, the Nicene Creed, the Agnus Dei and the Sanctus and Benedictus, have now departed from what used to be an ecumenical version of these texts generally used in the Church of England and previously in the Roman Catholic church.[19] Normally there were two priests in attendance, the celebrant wearing traditional Gothic-style vestments and a preacher wearing cassock, cotta and stole. Both priests would be wearing birettas on entrance. Besides Fr Stephen, there would normally be Fr Walter, a retired priest who has rooms in the vicarage, or the curate, Fr Thomas, about whom more will be said later. Much of the physical arrangements for the service are in the hands of a lay pastoral assistant. The Diocese of London has a scheme where prospective ordinands can spend a year working in a parish whilst exploring their vocations. During my time of research, there were three different pastoral assistants. The first one I met was of Polish origin. He went home on holiday and failed to return, announcing this via a brief text message to Fr Stephen. There had been no previous indication that this would happen, and he was in the process of moving towards training for ordination. Fr Stephen found this very upsetting. The second moved on to ordination training.

The service begins with the ringing of a bell and the singing of a hymn, during which the celebrant censes the altar. The hymn book used is *Celebration Hymnal*, a Roman Catholic compilation which includes a wide range of hymns, worship songs and choruses. After a brief welcome and introduction, there is a corporate act of penitence (the Confession) followed by absolution. The Gloria in Excelsis is sung followed by the Collect of the Day; this differs in text from that prescribed either in Common Worship or the Book of Common Prayer. Two scripture readings follow, with a psalm in between them. These are normally read by lay people. After these readings, there is a hymn followed by one of the priests reading the gospel. There is always a sermon of about eight minutes which is available in printed form after the service for worshippers to take away.

---

[19]   These texts were drawn up by the English Language Liturgical Consultation, an ecumenical group.

The Nicene Creed is then recited followed by intercessions. During the time that I was attending Holy Cross, it became usual practice for a lay person to lead these.[20] Fr Stephen felt that it was an opportunity to engage lay people in leading parts of the worship. The offertory follows whilst the celebrant prepares the altar and censes it. The Roman Rite Eucharistic Prayer was something I had not experienced. Two things struck me as being very different from the form of worship I am accustomed to. Before the consecration of the bread and wine, there is a section of short intercessions. Holy Cross followed the rite exactly by praying for "Francis, our Pope" (not Justin, Archbishop of Canterbury) and "Jonathan, our bishop" (the Area Bishop mentioned earlier who oversees traditionalist parishes in London). This was the pattern even before the Rt Revd Dame Sarah Mullally was appointed as Bishop of London. The second feature I found unusual was the Sharing of the Peace immediately after the consecration of the bread and wine. To me this is normally a time for quiet reflection, prayer and meditation, and I found it disconcerting that everyone was moving around and greeting each other. Silence followed as communion was administered. I noticed that, as in many Roman Catholic churches, not everyone went to the altar for communion or for a blessing. The service then ends with a blessing and a recessional hymn. Coffee, tea and cake are served afterwards at the back of the church, and about half the congregation usually stays for this, although it tends to be the older people who stay behind.

As I stated earlier, I found the complete use of the Roman Rite unusual, but it had been the practice at St Clement's for many years in spite of strictures by various bishops of London against its use, most recently by Bishop Richard Chartres in November 2011 when the new Roman Rite was being introduced.[21] Perhaps to counter this, and to avoid confusion, Holy Cross on its pew sheets and noticeboard describes itself as "The Anglican Church of The Holy Cross".

---

[20] I was asked to lead intercessions—the first lay person to do so—to show to the congregation that these could be led by a lay person.

[21] <https://www.churchtimes.co.uk/articles/2011/25-november/news/uk/chartres-using-roman-rite-is-serious-canonical-matter>, accessed 20 January 2023.

I referred earlier to there being a curate in post. I believe that this description is important as it shows how precarious is the relationship of some traditionalist Anglo-Catholic clergy with their ministries in the Church of England, as will be explained later. Fr Thomas had been at Holy Cross since June 2017 when he was ordained deacon, and we can see how he related to his position within the present Church of England and hence the possible attitude of Anglo-Catholics towards church planting. He was ordained priest by the Bishop of Fulham in June 2018 in St Clement's. I attended the service, which was a Common Worship ordination service, although within a traditional framework, i.e., an eastward-facing celebration of the Eucharist. This service showed that the ethnic diversity of the area was mirrored very much in the congregations of the two churches. (At Holy Cross, I estimate that about 75 per cent of the congregation were from an African-Caribbean background.) The ethnic diversity was very evident also in the food provided in the buffet afterwards, with Jamaican goat curry as the centrepiece. Fr Thomas continued his training as curate and regularly preached and celebrated the Eucharist at Holy Cross. His wife had a baby son in late November 2018. It therefore came as a great surprise to see him in the congregation (just wearing a cassock) on 24 February 2019. Before the service started, Fr Stephen announced that Fr Thomas was resigning his Anglican orders to join the Roman Catholic Church as a member of the Ordinariate.[22] A letter, jointly signed by the Bishop of Fulham and Fr Stephen, was handed out at the end of the Mass as a formal statement about this and also to inform those who were not at church that Sunday. When I interviewed Fr Stephen after I had finished my research visits, he expressed profound sadness and disappointment with Fr Thomas's decision, which had come as a complete surprise, especially considering his family circumstances. Fr Thomas's move does indicate the continuing unease of some traditionalist Anglo-Catholics with their position within the Church of England. There do not seem to be any official figures available for priests

---

[22]   The Personal Ordinariate of Our Lady of Walsingham was established in 2011 by Pope Benedict XVI to allow Anglicans to enter into the full communion of the Catholic Church whilst retaining much of their heritage and traditions. It now has the full support and blessing of Pope Francis.

who have joined the Roman Catholic Church either directly or through the Ordinariate. The number of priests at the time of writing who belong to the Ordinariate stands at 103, according to the clergy list on its website. Most of these joined shortly after the Ordinariate was founded. Professor Linda Woodhead in research carried out in 2014 established that 389 Catholic priests are former Anglican priests, including 87 priests in the Ordinariate of Our Lady of Walsingham.[23]

The reopening of Holy Cross for worship, in September 2010, was a step of faith by the then vicar and Fr Stephen, at that time his curate. To bring a building back into use for worship after 70 years of neglect is remarkable and very unusual in the Church of England. If it does happen, it is often the result of it being sold to another Christian denomination or even another faith. The church's "Mission Statement" says about Holy Cross:

> A smaller congregation that gathers for Mass at 5pm, seeking to remind the backstreets where we find ourselves that God loves them lots.[24]

The comment about the "backstreets" is so important in the demography of Holy Cross. Every Sunday an A-board is put outside announcing that Holy Cross is open for worship, so that there is local community visibility. On special occasions, such as when the bishop visits, the street outside is taken over by a bouncy castle to entertain the children whilst the adults have a glass of wine. Funding has been made available from the local Tesco Community Fund to improve the frontage, and at my last Sunday visit, plans were being drawn up to see how best that could be achieved.

Another way in which there is engagement with the community is a weekly lunch club on Tuesdays, mainly for older people; there is no charge, just a request for donations. This is preceded by Mass. Additionally there are Boys' Brigade groups for older children during the week. There is now church activity in the building on weekdays,

---

[23] <https://www.thetablet.co.uk/news/1028/new-figures-show-almost-400-catholic-priests-were-anglicans>, accessed 20 January 2023.

[24] From parish website, accessed 25 July 2020.

in addition to Sunday worship. Thus, Holy Cross is now again doing what its builders had in mind, being a sign of Christian presence in the southern part of the parish.

Conclusion

I had chosen Holy Cross as one of the churches to research as it stood firmly within the traditionalist part of Anglo-Catholicism.[25] Also because as a church plant, it was well established. I wanted to see if mission was still as important as it was in the nineteenth century when many Anglo-Catholic churches were built in London. I will discuss my conclusions in a subsequent chapter. For the moment, I need to place on record the important contribution that Fr Stephen has made to the success of the church. That he has been a constant feature in his parish for 12 years has given Holy Cross (and St Clement's) both a stability and a recognition in the neighbourhood as an important Christian presence. This was evidenced when I interviewed him over lunch in a local Italian restaurant. All through lunch people were coming up to him and greeting him—as well as asking how the new baby who had recently been born was progressing: a clear testament to incarnational ministry.

St Paul's Community Church, Melchester

I had driven up the M1 to this Midland city for the 3 p.m. service on 11 November 2018. When I reached the school where the service takes place, the car park was full, and cars were also parked on the double yellow lines outside. I had to park my car at a considerable distance away. I wondered what was happening. Then I saw Fr Sam, the Pioneer

---

[25]   The liberal versus traditionalist positions in Anglo-Catholicism are a relatively modern phenomenon originally brought about by the creation of the Church of South India in 1947. Many Anglo-Catholics held doubts about the validity of its priestly orders according to their understanding of the doctrine of Apostolic Succession. There was a church in the city where I was brought up which had a notice in its porch to the effect that members of the Church of South India were not welcome to receive communion.

Priest. I jokingly asked him if a revival was happening. Sadly not, was his reply, just a primary schools' football competition using the large sports area behind the school; but at least those who were attending could see that there was a church worshipping there. It is always difficult for a congregation worshipping in a secular building to make its presence obvious. The school entrance is in a side road which has only a few houses and is off the main road; all that can be seen of the school from the main road is a high and thick hawthorn hedge, hence Fr Sam's reliance on leafletting as a way of making the church's presence known.

The church and the background to the plant
This area of Melchester was until the mid-nineteenth century a typical Midlands village outside the county town. It was served by St Paul's, a twelfth-century church. As the population grew with increasing industrialization, especially the making of textiles, the city spread outwards and incorporated the village and the surrounding areas. Christ Church was opened in 1906, intentionally built in an art nouveau style to serve a growing working-class area of terraced housing and factories that characterized the surrounding streets. The area in which St Paul's Community Church is situated was previously in the separate parish of St Paul's—hence its name. The medieval Grade II parish church was the centre of worship for this village. However, over the years, the congregation decreased in size which necessitated a decision to close the church; it has not been used for worship since 2010. Since then, it has slowly been falling into disrepair and has been subjected to sporadic vandalism and break-ins. The building is on Historic England's "at risk" register because of its deteriorating state and people who live near the church, next to the river Mel, say they would like to see it brought back to some kind of sympathetic use. The Diocese of Melchester is currently looking to sell the disused St Paul's Church. A previous attempt to convert the building into an arts centre failed through lack of funding. The parish was also dissolved and divided between neighbouring parishes. The church school continued to keep the name of St Paul's, within the enlarged parish of Christ Church, but the relationship with Christ Church was relatively tenuous and for some time it was a "church school"

in name only.[26] As the school was running well, it became one of the lowest diocesan priorities.

This changed with the appointment of a new headteacher who was concerned that the church was not engaging in any realistic terms with one of its schools. By working with both the Diocesan Board of Education and the archdeacon and bishop of Melchester, a solution was found. Fr Sam was coming to the end of his licence as a university chaplain; he had a wide range of experience in different roles and was happy to accept the challenge of being a Pioneer Priest in this area. Although from a different churchmanship to that of Christ Church, he was attached to the parish both in terms of ministerial support and also to work with the school to ensure that it had a clear Christian presence and ethos. The diocese provided him with a house about three-quarters of a mile from the school, although physically in a different parish. Christ Church agreed to pay a fixed sum for expenses as the diocese was covering his stipend. Fr Sam is married, and his wife Mary supports him in his ministry. He has two teenage sons and a younger daughter who are all actively engaged in the church; in particular, they take charge of the laptop which is used to project worship songs and other supporting visual material.

Fr Sam started by using the Wednesday school assembly as a time of worship and began to include parents, carers and significant other adults. It became the regular service of worship for the community. However, it was soon realized that this was not a realistic long-term strategy because of pressure on school space and time. Although Fr Sam continues to lead the Wednesday assemblies, they are now just a part of normal school activity. It was therefore decided that the focus of community worship should be a service in the school hall at 3 p.m. on the second Sunday of the month in term time; this service began in September 2017. From September 2018 onwards this became a twice monthly service, although still only in term time because of the availability of the school hall. The school is situated on the other side of a main trunk road from the more recent housing development, with very few houses nearby. Although a

---

26   Information about St Paul's Community Church and its relationships both with the school, the Diocese of Melchester and the parish of Christ Church has been obtained through a number of conversations with Fr Sam.

school crossing patrol is in operation on weekdays to ensure the safety of children and parents, this does not operate on Sundays. The road as a result becomes a significant barrier and so may well affect the accessibility of the worship centre for those who live in these houses. Additionally, the road in which the school entrance is situated has a "bus only" bridge about a hundred yards away. If one wished to drive from the other side of the bridge, the detour is at least a mile in length. On the far side of the bridge is the disused parish church.

Fr Sam raised with me several times his view that church planting was easier in a newly built housing development than in an established community. That may be true if the priest is one of the first people to live in that development where he/she has a significant advantage, but in general this has not been found to be the case. Roger Lloyd describes the problems of housing estates in New Towns, but they are equally applicable to the estate that St Paul's School and Church serves. He writes: "although there were exceptions the Church plainly found the ... housing estate and the vast block of flats a field of ministry of peculiar and unexpected difficulty".[27] The area that St Paul's serves has the disadvantage of being relatively established although having the features of new town housing developments; hence the apparent lack of immediate impact on the community. Although Fr Sam was notionally attached to Christ Church and took services there, I saw no element of reciprocity, especially in terms of physical support for his work in visiting and community involvement. This became very clear when the Bishop's Mission Order was granted in June 2018, formally launching the church; the Vicar of Christ Church played no part in the service.[28]

About six months later, Fr Sam announced that Christ Church was ending its financial support of St Paul's as it wanted to employ a children's and families' worker and divert the funding to support this post. He said that the archdeacon was investigating other areas of support and

---

[27] Roger Lloyd, *The Church of England 1900–1965* (London: SCM Press, 1966).

[28] A Bishop's Mission Order (BMO) licenses a priest for work in a particular situation, either within an existing parish (but outside the control of the parish priest) or across a number of parishes. It is designed to relax some of the complex regulations around parishes and their boundaries.

funding. At the last service I attended in June 2019, Fr Sam told me that St Paul's was entering into a partnership from September 2019 with a large city centre Evangelical Anglican church, with a history of church planting. This church would provide £4,000 annually in funding for four years as well as commissioning six people, including a musician, to support St Paul's. He insisted that it was to be a partnership, not a takeover, which would enable the church to reach out more into the community with different forms of activities to supplement the Sunday worship; a foodbank was one such aim. He also wanted the informal style of worship to continue.

The church website describes the church in these words:

> We are Church but not a parish. The reason for this is complicated! We are located in the Parish of Christ Church, Melchester the largest parish and one of the most diverse parishes in the diocese. We are a Bishop's Mission Order which means that we have been set up by the Bishop as Church which can do things differently and has a special focus on Mission. We do things differently because we see that many people don't really 'get' traditional churches. Instead by focusing on people rather than organizations and buildings we try to be a church that anyone and everyone could be comfortable visiting. That's why we want to be a church for everyone. In particular we are a church that is especially welcoming to children and families. A lot of our members have children who attend our school but you don't need to have children at the school to worship with us. We are a Church which is home to a number of people with disabilities and always happy to welcome more.[29]

This vision is one that Fr Sam is very keen to maintain and enhance.

As noted earlier, the church meets in the school hall. It is a barren and utilitarian space, but work is in hand to make it more attractive for worship. There is already an altar (designed by the schoolchildren and donated by a benefactor), and Fr Sam wants a number of frontals

---

[29]   Accessed 27 July 2020.

to reflect the liturgical seasons. At least one of these has already been designed and completed.

Fr Sam believes that symbols and colour are more important than words and therefore hopes that people in this locality will respond to this. Such artefacts can only enhance worship; this clearly resonates with the ideas of the nineteenth-century Anglo-Catholics. Another example was when, at Pentecost, he draped large areas of the space with red cloth, symbolizing the descent of the Holy Spirit. There is even a tentative proposal to put some stained glass in the clerestory windows, to bring even more colour into the building. The school is very supportive of these ideas.

Statistical data
St Paul's is located in the parish of Christ Church, one of the largest in Melchester, both in area and in terms of population, to the north of the city. The data is for the parish as a whole as it is not possible to define clearly the area served by St Paul's and so extract the relevant data.

St Paul's Community Church—population and age profile

Deprivation	Population	Area (Sq. Miles)	Density
1200	48263	2.9	15361

%0–4	%5–17	%18–29	%30–44	%45–64	%65+
7.2	17.00	20.3	20.8	23.5	11.2

St Paul's Community Church—ethnicity (%)

White	Asian	Black	Mixed	Other
23.0	64.7	7.2	2.6	2.6

St Paul's Community Church—religion profile (%)

Christian	Buddhist	Hindu	Jewish
18.0	0.3	44.0	0.0

Muslim	Sikh	Other	None
18.0	5.0	0.8	9.8

Not Stated	4.1

It can easily be seen from the data that Christianity is very much a minority religion in the parish. It is also to be noted that the number of respondents who claim to have no religion is very low, as is the number of those who did not respond to that particular census question. Both of these figures are lower than the English average as recorded in the 2011 census. On the surface, therefore, it would seem that the parish has a high level of religious observance. Because of the location of St Paul's and the pattern of the main roads, other places of worship were not easily identifiable in the area.

Worship at St Paul's
The chairs are laid out in a semi-circle in the school facing the altar on which usually there is one lighted candle. When I was attending, the services were all non-eucharistic, so the altar just provided a focal point. To the right of the altar is a large interactive projection screen on which the words of the songs are displayed. There is a loose format for the service, but it is not slavishly followed. Fr Sam does not wear robes to lead worship, just his normal day clothes and his clerical collar. He is known in the school by the way he dresses, usually in distinctively coloured trousers, shirt and jumper. This is a deliberate choice on his part as he wants at the same time to be ordinary, or eccentric, but also be marked out for his calling.

When Fr Sam thinks most people have arrived, anything up to ten minutes after the advertised time, he starts by going round the group and asking if they have any good news or something to share. This is quite easy as there were never more than 20 in attendance, adults and children, including Fr Sam's family, and often far fewer.[30] He also takes orders for tea and coffee, which will be served later during the service. Then a song is sung. Fr Sam uses children's worship songs from various American websites. They all involve actions, and for the most part, everyone joins

---

[30] During the time I attended, it was noticeable that only two other adults, other than Fr Sam's family, were present at every service; one worked at the school as a teaching assistant, the other, an older mother, came with her autistic son. She said that she felt welcomed and comfortable as no-one judged or criticized the unpredictable behaviour of her son.

in. There is a very limited repertoire, but that does not seem to concern people. One song, "My God is a great big God", seemed to be sung virtually every time I attended, as was "Jesus Christ, my lighthouse". These songs involved actions, joined in with enthusiasm by the members of the congregation. Fr Sam then introduces the theme for the service, sometimes with a short Bible reading or story. This comes out of one of the lectionary readings for the day, usually the gospel reading. There is often a short time of discussion, but this is dependent on numbers. He then introduces some form of craft activity relevant to the theme. Mary, his wife, does all the organization and preparation for this with the help of their children. (Given the usual reticence of many teenagers to be visibly Christians, it was good to see their two teenage sons being actively and enjoyably involved.) This is also the time for tea, coffee and cake. This has been a feature of St Paul's from the very start and stresses the informality of the church and fits in to some degree with "Café Church", which is one of the popular varieties of Fresh Expressions. Some of the adults join in the craft activity, particularly helping the smaller children. This time gives Fr Sam an opportunity to engage with adults on a personal basis and so begin to build relationships. This part of the service takes about half an hour. Fr Sam then asks the children to say something about the craft activity, and he relates it back to his theme. One or two more songs are sung, and the service ends with a short prayer and a reminder of when the next service will be.

This informal style of worship was very alien to me, and I found it quite difficult to engage with it as worship. I had to take notes so that I could have a good recollection of what was taking place. However, I can appreciate how it could appeal to people whose contact with church is through church primary school assemblies which often offer the same style of informal music and interaction. The use of a familiar building also takes away some of the discomfort that new worshippers often find in attempting to enter a traditional church building. This style of worship is also helpful in engaging with people who do not speak English as a first language, as there is opportunity to ask questions if things are not easily grasped, rather than enduring what might be, for them, a totally incomprehensible liturgy. I noticed this on a number of occasions both with an Asian family and with a Polish woman who spoke very little English and was accompanied by two mixed-race children.

My choice of St Paul's as a research site was influenced by two particular factors; firstly, I wanted a site outside of London, particularly as London is seen as different in religious terms from most other parts of the United Kingdom.[31] Secondly, I wanted to research a church plant that was completely new and not building on something of the past. This church plant did arise within an Anglo-Catholic parish, but I do not believe that there was originally any thought-out intentionality on the part of the parish. It came into being as a result of an initiative from the church school in the parish which was then taken up by the diocesan authorities as an opportunity to enhance the mission of the Church in that part of Melchester, especially as the original place of worship had been closed in 2010. However, the parish benefited by having an additional priest to share the workload, especially on Sunday mornings. But the fact that after less than two years the parish withdrew the financial support seems in my view to provide some evidence of this lack of commitment and intentionality.

Post-research follow-up

Given the change of sponsorship that was to take place after I had finished my research visits, I decided that a follow-up conversation with Fr Sam would be useful to ensure that my research reflected the most recent reality. I therefore had a conversation with him, via Zoom, in early August 2020. This conversation took place during the Covid-19 pandemic and schools had been closed for more than four months. I reminded Fr Sam of his earlier words that the relationship with the new sponsoring church would be a partnership, rather than a takeover. His reply was that it had become in reality more of a takeover, although there had been some positive aspects as well. However, heavily influenced by the enforced

---

[31] See David Goodhew and Anthony-Paul Cooper (eds), *The Desecularisation of the City* (Abingdon: Routledge, 2019) for an analysis of this phenomenon.

closure of the school, which has meant the suspension of worship, he has asked the archdeacon to "pause the partnership and review it".

As noted above, the style of worship was very informal, a deliberate decision when St Paul's opened; a key aspect of this was that children and adults stayed together for the whole service. This is made clear on the website. With the influx of the team of helpers from the sponsoring church, its vicar felt that the worship was on too superficial a level. He wanted a more structured service, beginning with a time of singing (seemingly synonymous with worship); the children would then leave for Sunday School activities in one of the classrooms, whilst the adults listened to a sermon of at least ten minutes in length. This was to be followed by some form of discussion and prayer. The previous attenders at the church objected to the proposed changes, and Fr Sam supported their views. The complaint from the new sponsoring church was that things were moving too slowly in building a congregation. Fr Sam's view was that there was a need to build up relationships within the community first. There are here, in my view, two distinct evangelistic models at play which are in opposition to each other. An example of this came at Christmas. Fr Sam, with the support of resources from the new sponsor, arranged a number of activities. Every house in the area was personally visited with an invitation. There was a good attendance. Fr Sam was pleased that he had met a number of new people and been able to show them that the church was there and accessible for them. Those from the sponsoring church wanted to collect contact details so that their visiting team could arrange follow-up home visits, which was not the way in which Fr Sam saw his relationships with those who attended the church. It was tensions such as these that led Fr Sam to ask the archdeacon to review the arrangements. Then the "lockdown" intervened.[32] At the time of my research, St Paul's was in a state of suspension with an uncertain future.

There are also a number of external factors that will have a significant influence on the future of St Paul's. Fr Sam was appointed as a Pioneer Priest by the previous bishop who saw full-time ordained pioneers as the

---

[32]   One area of agreement between the two clergy was that an Alpha course would not work at St Paul's as "Alpha is too posh".

way forward. Fr Sam is the only one of those still in post. The new bishop has a very different model: that pioneer work should be undertaken by lay people with the support of a facilitator—a parish priest who is given one day a week to support these pioneers. Fr Sam's position is therefore now seen as anomalous in the diocese.

The Diocese of Melchester, like many dioceses in the Church of England, is under increasing financial strain, which has been exacerbated by Covid-19 and the extended closure of churches. It has already decided to leave posts unfilled when clergy leave. In addition, the Bishop's Mission Order will expire in less than two years, which will lead to a review. This has implications for the future of St Paul's as to whether it will be allowed to continue in its present form with a full-time pioneer stipendiary priest. There are a number of possible scenarios, one of which is that the sponsoring church takes it over completely and adds it to the other plants it supports elsewhere in the city. Fr Sam could then be offered one of a number of vacant parishes. Nothing has been agreed as yet, but (at the time of writing) there are signs that St Paul's will not be able to continue in its current form post-Covid-19.[33] There are significant problems about the use of the school if the enhanced practices in respect of intensive cleaning have to be maintained—yet another uncertainty of which account needs to be taken.

General conclusion

In this chapter, I have attempted to give a picture of the three churches: both of their geographical and demographic situations, and of their main Sunday service, which is still the most prominent public face of the church and its major form of interaction with the parish at large. If the Sunday service is not seen as uplifting, spiritually helpful or lacking

---

[33] It was reported on the church's Facebook page in May 2021 that Fr Sam was standing down. In a personal email, Fr Sam referred to the tensions involved in the new partnership as well as wider moves regarding clergy deployment in the diocese. These had influenced his decision.

in a sense of welcome, worshippers soon lose interest and fall away.[34] This applies not only to Anglo-Catholic churches but to all styles of worship. However, the reason that I have described the services in such detail is that the pioneers of the Oxford Movement wanted worship to be conducted reverently in a way that was honouring to God. As such, even before the advent of ritualism, one of the key aspects of their worship was a strict adherence to the rubric and words of the Prayer Book. This was very much in contrast to the way in which worship was being conducted in many churches of that time. In many cases, services had become casual and chaotic, as Thomas Hardy humorously describes.[35] The descriptions of worship show how far these churches fulfilled what the Oxford Movement pioneers would have wanted. These descriptions will also help the reader to understand that church planting in an Anglo-Catholic context is not monochrome, but that each plant originates in a specific context and therefore develops according to that context.

In the following chapters, I will look at some of the features of these churches and the lessons that can be drawn from their different experiences in order to find important factors to support Anglo-Catholic church planting.

---

[34] I use the word "service" to include not only the worship element but the whole ethos surrounding it.

[35] Thomas Hardy provided comical descriptions of the church band and throughout his life appreciated the formality of High Church worship. See Jan Jedrzejewski, *Thomas Hardy and The Church* (London: Palgrave Macmillan, 1996), Chapter 3.

5

Emerging themes from research

The starting point of any research analysis is the research question that underpins the activity. My aim was to investigate current church planting within the Anglo-Catholic wing of the Church of England and compare it with the way in which Anglo-Catholics established new churches in the nineteenth century. This would allow me to establish both similarities and differences, as well as to investigate what could be learned from those experiences that might be relevant today. This double focus was chosen to evidence a broad range of Anglo-Catholic experience both from participant observation and from historical sources. It would show some kind of continuum of practice and that church planting for Anglo-Catholics was not just a new fad.

A researcher must always have in the front of his/her mind the question: "What exactly am I looking for and seeking to evidence through this research?" Specifically, it means trying to ascertain the distinctiveness of church planting in an Anglo-Catholic context. Does it differ in essence and practice from the more common, and the usual, Evangelical models, referred to earlier as described by Michael Moynagh and Philip Harrold?[1]

---

[1]   Michael Moynagh with Philip Harrold, *Church for Every Context: An Introduction to Theology and Practice* (London: SCM Press, 2012), pp. 206–20.

The six themes

The themes that I have identified through my participant observation and from the literature around church planting are broad in scope, as is to be expected when analysing three distinct churches. They are also factors that need to be taken into account by any church, not just Anglo-Catholic churches, when considering church planting. It is also not possible to rank them, as what is the most important theme for one church is not necessarily the same for the others because of the different contexts in which they operate. That being said, the themes of *worship* and *community*, which are usually regarded as important marks of a church, stand out. These are the six themes:

- **Worship** Under this heading I also include the concepts of *spirituality* and *beauty*. As will be seen later, each church had a different approach and emphasis, but all of them laid great importance on its regular act of worship. This is not surprising as worship, and especially the regular celebration of the Eucharist, has been and still is one of the key expressions of Anglo-Catholicism.
- **Community** This also encompasses *welcome* and *mission*. Again, each church saw this in a different way and therefore interpreted community differently. The varied natures of the parishes also influenced this. Involvement with the community of the parish is again an important part of Anglo-Catholic ecclesiology as has been seen in an earlier chapter, with its stress on the incarnational ministry of the priest in the parish. There is often a tension between ministry to the worshipping community, almost akin to chaplaincy, and ministry to the wider community, and some churchgoers resent the latter, especially when they believe that they are paying, via the Diocesan Parish Share Scheme, for *their* vicar. The classic Church of England position is that "the cure of souls" by the parish priest, and shared with the bishop, relates to all who live in the geographical parish. This is affirmed by the

bishop every time a priest is licensed or instituted into a new benefice.[2]

- **Vision** This is linked to leadership as the leader carries forward the vision, but that vision may have initially come from elsewhere, e.g., the diocese, another church, a predecessor. Vision is the outworking of intentionality by identifying what needs to be put into place to fulfil the intention that "the church needs to do something about this". The vision is developed, and the leader carries it forward with support.

- **Leadership** This theme was identified not only by each of the priests but also by their congregations. In my informal encounters over coffee, many commented on the way in which Father X was leading the way forward for them. This is not to say that others were not involved, but they depended on his clear leadership and drive. It is important to note that this is not management, a concept which I thought I might find mentioned, but did not in fact emerge.

- **Growth** Each of the churches had a desire to grow within the physical limitations of their premises. Growth also meant for all of them an increasing contact with their wider communities—not just regular churchgoers.

- **Sustainability** This was an issue raised by the clergy, rather than members of the congregations. The question generally concerns what happens if the priest leaves. Members of congregations, in my experience as a Deanery Lay Chair and hence involved with the process of filling clergy vacancies for more than 30 years, do not address this issue until their priest's departure is announced. Is the church which Father X led now able to continue without him? If so, what will his replacement be like? What changes will the new vicar make? This is an important factor and is addressed at length by Moynagh and Harrold.[3] It also presupposes that the diocesan administration is able to support parishes in a speedy

---

[2]   *Bishop: N.* receive the Cure of Souls which is both yours and mine; in the name of the Father, and of the Son, and of the Holy Spirit. *Incumbent:* Amen.

[3]   Moynagh with Harrold, *Church for Every Context*, pp. 411ff.

process of recruitment and also potentially in the management of change—a resource which in most cases is sadly lacking. As a result, sustainability is often not seen as a priority and there is the myth, and in some dioceses the reality, that vacancies are extended for financial reasons.[4] Clergy vacancies have their challenges for every congregation, but in a church plant, which often does not have a significant supporting infrastructure or mature lay leaders, a gap of any length of time in the leadership of the plant can be fatal.

Reporting the research findings

In this section, I intend to look at each of the themes in relation to each church and use quotations from interviews and questionnaires to show how these themes are worked out in each of them.

Worship, spirituality and beauty

This theme is an important element in Anglo-Catholicism as has been noted previously and taken up by R. F. Littledale in 1868 in his description of London gin palaces.[5]

St Pancras, Rushey Common
This broader concept was seen by Fr Francis as a key part of the ministry of his church. Although he sees liturgy as important, he says: "Liturgy is not enough if it's not rooted in contemplation." As described in an earlier chapter, the liturgy at St Pancras, although Anglo-Catholic, does not have the full range of liturgical ceremonial that takes place in its sponsoring church, St Paul's. Respondent 3 to the questionnaire,

---

[4]   With the church plant in my own parish, the previous priest left at the end of January and his replacement was in post by Easter—an unusually short vacancy.

[5]   The original of this quotation from Littledale is to be found in John Shelton Reed, *Glorious Battle: The Cultural Politics of Victorian Anglo-Catholicism* (Nashville, TN: Nashville University Press, 1996), p. 150.

who came from a Methodist background, appreciated "[The] form of service, music, friendly atmosphere". This was echoed by Respondent 8 who appreciated the "prayerful worship". Fr Francis's emphasis on contemplation is something that underpins everything that he does and is important in his celebration of the liturgy, rather than the externals. He commented that in his view "the Anglo-Catholic world has a preoccupation with vestments". I interpret this statement as his concern about an overemphasis on the externals of worship, sometimes at the expense of the spiritual dimension. The early Anglo-Catholics had the same concerns, and many were uncomfortable with these externals. Pickering comments that ritual is of no value and is a vain thing if it is not based upon sound doctrine.[6] This is the view of Fr Francis as he believes that spirituality and the contemplative life are part of "the true, authentic and real Catholic tradition" and that "the contemplative tradition is such a huge part of our lives". Hence, he wants his church to be a centre for mindfulness and spirituality as one of the foundations of its mission. In his view, "rooting this Centre in the Catholic tradition, really, and I think that all the great mystics as well as the desert fathers and mothers can give us a lot about this and we can actually revitalize the Anglo-Catholic tradition from a very new perspective". He sees that "if there isn't that contemplative attention in our lives, the major risk is that we can water down the mission; yes, and water down and empty the Anglo-Catholic tradition. We all become social workers." Yet he realizes that there must be a balance: "yes we have to keep a balanced attention to, well, social justice and [the]spiritual journey". This is summed up by Respondent 1 who loved "the peace" and Respondent 2 who referred to "the lovely church atmosphere".

Holy Cross, Greystone
The background to the founding of Holy Cross defines very well the style of worship. As an in-parish plant using a parish-owned resource, it was much more likely to reflect the traditional Anglo-Catholic style of worship of the parish church. This was very clear from my research

---

[6]   W. S. F. Pickering, *Anglo-Catholicism: A Study in Religious Ambiguity* (London: Routledge, 1989), p. 21.

visits when I saw both the use of the Roman Breviary for Evening Prayer and the Roman Rite of the Mass. I asked Fr Stephen whether the Roman Missal had always been used as far as he knew. He referred to a priest who had died in post in 1986 and who used the Alternative Service Book with Roman additions.[7] Referring to old stencils of Holy Week services that he had found in the vicarage attic, he said, "They were quite literally ASB with bits of Roman Missal stuck into it." Certainly, when his predecessor, who was instrumental in reopening Holy Cross, had come to St Clement's in 1994, the Roman Missal was the established liturgy in use. He commented that at funerals, which generally took the form of a Requiem Mass, "that's where the Roman Catholics are surprised". He also spoke about the time that the new English translation of the Roman Missal was introduced in Advent 2011. There were significant changes of wording; for example, the response to "The Lord be with you" was changed from "and also with you" to the more archaic "and with thy spirit". There were also changes to other texts including the "Gloria in Excelsis" and the Nicene Creed. He said: "I had to be quite open about why the rite was changing, why we use the Roman Rite." He was also clear that "when we opened Holy Cross, I didn't want it to be a watered-down version of St Clement's". Fr Stephen is conscious of the limitations imposed by the size of Holy Cross as "having more than 60 people in that building is quite difficult". There was a tension, especially for those families bringing children for baptisms, between using a functional building like Holy Cross, where they normally worshipped, and a larger, more traditional and elaborate building like St Clement's. However, Fr Stephen was insistent that "we wanted there to be permanent elements to the church so that it wasn't bringing the altar out on wheels". This was very clear from my participant observation. The altar was set on a raised platform at one end of the building. A tabernacle for the Reserved Sacrament was situated on a window ledge above the altar. On either side there were statues, one of Jesus and the other of the Virgin

---

[7]   Usually referred to as the ASB and introduced into the Church of England in 1980 after a number of experimental liturgies, known as Series 1, Series 2 and Series 3. It ceased to be authorized for use when it was replaced by *Common Worship* in 2000.

Mary. There was also a votive candle stand. The chairs were moveable, but the artefacts connected with worship were fixed. This very much reflected a traditional style of Anglo-Catholic worship which was further emphasized both by the wearing of birettas by the clergy and by the style of the vestments, especially the fiddle-back chasuble, so typical of the late-nineteenth-century ritualist Anglo-Catholics. The only thing that prevented the Mass from being fully traditional was that the Eucharist was celebrated from behind the altar, facing the people: "westward facing" rather than "eastward facing" (*ad orientem*) with the priest's back to the people. I felt that this was a concession to the narrowness of the platform on which the altar stood, a pragmatic arrangement rather than a liturgical statement. Respondent 14 summed up the worship and atmosphere of Holy Cross when responding to the question "What do you like about the church?" She answered: "sermons, spiritual feeling, closeness to God".

St Paul's Community Church, Melchester
Given that this church meets in a school hall with a very informal style of worship, I was surprised at many of the comments made by Fr Sam. He first commented that the very informal style of worship "does create a lot of additional work" when compared to leading a service using a written liturgical resource such as Common Worship. But the most important of his comments referred to "beauty". He referred to the first occasion when the vicar of the new sponsoring church, All Saints, a large charismatic Evangelical church, visited. He showed him the altar and the frontal that the children of the school had designed with its colours and pictures. He continues: "I said about the colours and the message, and I thought, you know, my primary reason was to flag up something. Yes, and I said to him, you know that I think some models of mission are too verbal, too wordy, yes too written wordy . . . I talked about colour and beauty. Yeah, and feeling particularly brave I talked about the first generation of Anglo-Catholics . . . I've been hugely influenced by them and to my mind they were much more mission-minded than I think the second generation was, so I could have been in the first generation." He went on to say that he was in a working-class parish and that he wanted to bring something of heaven in, "not a man standing at the front, you know, whispering

matins, but actually a communion service with light and colour". His wish was that when they started a foodbank or a debt advice service, those coming to these would feel they were coming into a building with something different—not just a typical boring school hall. This theme he repeated several times during the course of our conversation and referred to "a theology of look heavenly, very different from what you are currently living".[8] There needs to be "some incultural and missional thinking that is slightly different". I found this concept of beauty and the expression of worship through visual stimuli to be very refreshing. How it will work out alongside the currently informal style of worship and in what is a basic school multi-use hall is the challenge for Fr Sam, especially as he works with a new supporting church which finds such concepts quite alien.

Throughout this section the contrasts in the interpretation of this theme by these three churches have been very apparent. Worship is conditioned by the physical space available as well as by the underlying personality and the theological and liturgical views of each priest. What can be seen is that the Anglo-Catholic concepts of the externals that underpin the act of worship can be interpreted today in a variety of ways, and so cannot be constrained by a "one-size-fits-all" approach; and they are heavily influenced by differing factors over which a priest and congregation often have little control.

Community, welcome and mission

Each of the churches emphasized this aspect as being a very important part of their *raison d'être*, and this was reflected both in the intentionality of the priest as well as in the responses to the questionnaires. Welcome and acceptance are essential components of mission and the building of community: both the community of the church and the secular community are outworkings of the gospel.[9]

---

[8] Living on a bleak 1960s council estate in north Melchester.

[9] Ephesians 2:19 (NRSV) "members of the household of God"; Jeremiah 29:7 (NRSV) "seek the welfare of the city . . . and pray to the Lord on its behalf, for in its welfare you will find your welfare".

St Pancras, Rushey Common

Fr Francis sees his mission as focussed on a number of different communities. He wants his church to grow "by responding to the needs of the local community but also to the wider needs of the city". He recognized that his was a welcoming congregation as well as a diverse one in terms of its (mainly white) ethnicity: "This diversity, I think it's distinctive in the Anglo-Catholic tradition and in my view should be especially in this city[10] . . . I think that's where we're going, and we need to keep it. We need to make it grow and be more and more inclusive . . . it makes our mission very distinctive." He then referred to French and Italian people with whom he was in contact. He said that they had previously given up churchgoing, but were now coming back, because "sometimes it's just they're looking for something else". Importantly he recognizes that the people—the church community—makes the church, not the priest alone. He sees the importance of the need "to concentrate on connecting with people's lives, yes, real lives, the pain, the joy, the suffering". He related an incident where a French family started to attend church because one of their sons was a friend of his son. This boy said that if Michael goes to church it must be fun, so the family started to attend and the children enjoyed the Sunday School activities. Fr Francis sees the Sunday School as an important means of mission. This is an interesting link with what Richard Temple West saw as important at St Mary Magdalene, Paddington. Through the attendance of the children, Fr Francis wants to build a solid group of parents. My observations confirmed that and especially the confident and articulate way in which the children told the adults what they had been doing and what they had learned. This family environment and welcome is an important factor, but it is not at the expense of inclusivity. It is also in the context of what I would describe as "lived evangelism" rather than overt preaching. He recounts a parent saying to him "you didn't try to convert me, I felt you weren't talking about salvation and 'you're going to hell'".

This approach is clearly evidenced in the questionnaire responses. One of the questions asked: "What do you like about the church?" Respondent

---

[10]   London is generally reckoned to be the most ethnically diverse city in the United Kingdom.

2, a middle-aged woman, replied: "Lovely church atmosphere, small congregation, has been very supportive personally." This was mirrored by Respondent 6, a middle-aged man: "The sense of community, hospitality and the energy of Fr Francis"; and a younger woman, Respondent 11, who had previously attended a very rural church in the north of England, said: "Friendly and informal and many opportunities to get involved in the community." Other respondents liked the fact that the church "was child-friendly".

The importance of this theme to St Pancras cannot be overstressed. It is built into the original vision of using the building in the service of the community, and I certainly experienced that welcome, that warmth, on all of my visits.

Holy Cross, Greystone
Given that Holy Cross is a plant in a different part of the parish from the parish church as well as being, in church planting terms, well established, it is not surprising that this theme is evident in its activities, from the use of part of the building by community groups to the weekly church-sponsored Tuesday lunch. Fr Stephen believes strongly in being visible as the parish priest and this carries over into the worshipping life of the church. He put it like this: "I think if you create a culture whereby, for example, that you say hello to Father when you pass on the highway, it's a bit easier when Granny dies to mention that." This sense of welcoming acceptance was evident in the church. He personally welcomed people as they came in, up to three minutes before the time of the service. He engaged with them and was able to focus on any concerns that they had, e.g., a sick relative.

He related to me what he regarded as an amazing incident about a boy who used to attend the Boys' Brigade meetings: "I remember one of them, he must be about 25 now. He's off work with depression and hasn't worked for months. He was in our Boys' Brigade and never really came to Mass, but then suddenly rocked up at a midweek Mass at St Clement's . . . He said, 'I remember you saying that there was a Mass every day, and so I thought there must be one today' . . . I was flabbergasted that something I had said maybe eight years ago when he was in the Boys' Brigade had stuck with him, such that he came to Mass on that Wednesday morning."

This again shows the value of welcome and community involvement and being "with" people, as well as the positive impact of a long-term ministry. This theme comes across in the responses to the questionnaire. Respondent 8, a priest who had retired to the area, referred to "Friendly and welcoming congregation and good ministry of word and sacrament." An older woman, Respondent 2, mentioned "the love shown to us" and Respondent 14, in the same age group, spoke of "Sermons, community family element, spiritual feeling, closeness to God." Fr Stephen summed it up in these words: "it's about being genuine, I think, yes, come and join me. It's a powerful message which places like HTB have got very well."

I felt very strongly that welcome and mission, especially in terms of the Anglo-Catholic view of incarnational ministry, were strongly emphasized at Holy Cross. I experienced this each time I attended when I joined in the coffee after Mass as well as being included on the rota for reading and leading intercessions.

St Paul's Community Church, Melchester
The fact that the word "community" is in the church's title shows that it places its emphasis on the community of the church school and the surrounding area that it serves. From my many informal conversations with Fr Sam I had already learned of his engagement with the local community and his efforts to welcome them into the church, especially after the move, noted earlier, from Wednesday to Sunday worship. He also had delivered leaflets to invite people to special services. But it was very much a sole effort, although as at Holy Cross, it was the priest being visible around the neighbourhood with his own distinctive, although idiosyncratic, dress.

The change of sponsorship has certainly released more resources to support community involvement. As Fr Sam said, "in terms of outreach, with a larger team, there's a lot more outreach. So, for example, one of the things I've often thought is that we should do some community work. Thanks to All Saints where basically it's taken about three phone calls, we've got a foodbank. This is the sort of thing that again focuses us out." He goes on to mention the difficulties of being a lone worker and the safety issues involved.[11] He continued by suggesting that having more resources both for visiting and practical activities in the community like litter clearing would be great and people from St Paul's could join in with those from All Saints who had committed to support. With the help of All Saints, both a foodbank and a money advice service were set up. But from informal conversations again, which were the result of the relationship I had built with Fr Sam and his family, he told me that there were tensions in the differing approaches to outreach. The example he gave was of the Christmas Carol Services. Those who were supporting from All Saints wanted to take contact details of everyone who came so that the "follow-up team" could do its work by home visitation, which he saw as in the nature of "hard sell" evangelism. For his own part, Fr Sam wanted to add the names to his contact list so that he could keep in touch with them and invite them to special services. The contrasts between different strategies of mission became quite apparent. I observed the way in which Fr Sam came alongside those who attended the service and gently spoke to them about what issues or problems they had and what the church could offer in support.[12] Fr Sam's sense of mission and community, especially in this very working-class area, is summed up in this comment about the first generation Anglo-Catholics: "as one chap said, I'd much rather go to the East End where the gospel is more unknown than in Bombay". He had always wanted to run a holiday club for the local children.[13] All Saints had in previous years been involved in one as part of a national charismatic Evangelical network. The question arose whether there would be one for All Saints and a separate one,

---

[11] Note here that Jesus sent out The Seventy in pairs; they needed mutual support but also mutual protection: Luke 10:1ff.

[12] It is worth commenting that many people in all of our churches need practical support of various kinds. As an example, I recently helped the wife of a couple (the husband had dementia) negotiate the paperwork of selling their bungalow and buying a flat. Is this a neglected area of mission?

[13] A Christian-based activity for children that usually takes place over a period of several days during school summer holidays.

involving people from St Paul's in their building. The question was unresolved at the end of my research.[14]

As mentioned earlier, because of very low attendance, by the time I wanted to introduce the questionnaire, the response rate was exceptionally poor. However, in spite of this it is worth quoting the responses that I received. Respondent 1 said: "It is very friendly people, and we enjoy it." It is interesting to note that this woman is Indian and married to a Polish man. Her grasp of English is quite elementary, but she values what St Paul's provides for her and her children, especially in the area of biblical education. Respondent 2 said: "My son has special needs, and he's understood and welcomed, not judged." I had met this woman every time I attended. Her son was very hyperactive and unpredictable in his behaviour, and I can imagine how difficult it would have been for a more formal and structured church to cope with his behaviour.

There are significant present and potential tensions in the relationship between St Paul's and All Saints. A researcher cannot solve them, nor attempt to do so, however attractive this course of action may be, but in the midst of these challenges, there is clear evidence of mission, welcome and community.

Vision

I have already quoted the scriptural statement "where there is no vision, the people perish". For any church plant to succeed there needs to be a vision, a plan, a strategy of what the intended outcome should be. In the case of St Pancras, this was clearly set out in the plan to link it with St Paul's which has been described earlier. For Holy Cross, it was a matter of taking a positive decision to use an existing, but virtually forgotten, resource as a way of extending the outreach of the parish church into a different area of the parish. In the case of St Paul's Community Church, the strategy arose via discussions between the diocese, the school and the parish church, but there were seemingly no clearly defined aims

---

[14]   There is a temptation in research to want to continue. There must be a *terminus post quem*, otherwise the research findings can never be finalized—much as the researcher might want to continue involvement. I leave it for future researchers to follow this through.

and objectives.[15] Hence the problems which arose later. A plant cannot be sustained *in vacuo*. The parables of the building of the tower or the king waging war warn Christians against a lack of planning for mission (Luke 14:28–33). Any church plant must have some kind of vision, some intentionality, towards what it wants to become in the context in which it is set.

St Pancras, Rushey Common
For Fr Francis, the vision for St Pancras which was developed in conjunction with the Vicar of St Paul's had as its main focus to ensure that the church became a lively, accessible place of worship which offered much to the community. One strand of this was: "we wanted St Pancras to be a centre for mindfulness and spirituality, but we didn't really know what we meant. Now we have a centre for spirituality where people can learn meditation . . . So, during the vision, I was trying to shape the vision as we had an intuition of what was the future."

An important part of the vision for a church plant is that there must be wide ownership and acceptance. If the leader does not share the vision with others, it is most likely to fail. Fr Francis "took the vision to the people. We brought them into the vision and said this is what we are going to do—and nobody objected." This was in contrast to a priest he mentioned who decided that he wanted to have a new parish hall, but he did not have a vision, only a project. He took this project to his PCC, which rejected the idea. Fr Francis described his way of working and sharing the vision like this: "I talk to people all the time, not just the churchwardens . . . I engage with them and say this is what I've got in mind. What do you think? And that is important because sometimes you just don't know. They tell you, look, this doesn't work; so, you don't waste your time and you're engaging with them."

The clarity of Fr Francis's vision and his keen engagement across both his own congregation and that at St Paul's has enabled this vision to bear fruit. The Centre for Mindfulness and Spirituality is in action, running

---

15   In any missional activity—among which I count church planting—it is vital to have a clear understanding of what is to be achieved, with markers against which to evaluate progress.

a variety of courses including a "Children and Family" course which includes yoga. There also has been a course which links mindfulness with creative writing. Fr Francis has also set up a separate website to introduce the Centre. The homepage states:

> We are a group of Christian and Non-Christian persons who are passionate about Mindfulness and Spirituality. As part of our vision at St Pancras we wish to answer to the needs of our Local community by promoting St Pancras Church as a Centre for Mindfulness and Spirituality. Deeply rooted in the Christian Tradition of meditation and contemplation, the St Pancras Centre encourages the participants to the different courses to learn the contemplative practice as a skill and as a discipline that helps open doorways to live in the present moment.[16]

This explains how the vision has materialized and is a key part of the mission of St Pancras to its parish and further afield. The concept of mindfulness is criticized in some Christian circles as "new age" or a practice of Buddhism and on a par with yoga, which draws on Hindu spirituality. Fr Francis insists that it fits in with the authentic meditative tradition which has been a practice of the Church from the early Desert Fathers and through Ignatian Spirituality to the present day.

Holy Cross, Greystone

The original vision which set up Holy Cross came from Fr Stephen's predecessor as Vicar of St Clement's, although Fr Stephen was the curate who took responsibility for the reopening of Holy Cross as a place of worship. However, there is still the need for an ongoing vision. Fr Stephen sees it in terms of ensuring that Holy Cross has its own independent congregation. He describes the churchgoers in the parish as being in three groups: those who attend St Clement's for the Sunday morning Mass; those who attend either St Clement's or Holy Cross, as convenient; and the group that only worships at Holy Cross. This is a growing group. His

---

16 I have not provided a reference as this would breach the convention of anonymity.

vision is that this group continues to grow. He also wants Holy Cross "to establish itself as a place where things like that [baptisms] or occasional offices happen". This fits in with his aim "to try to continue to make Holy Cross feel as much as a proper church as possible so that it doesn't end up the poor relation". Allied to this is the need for financial stability both for Holy Cross and the parish as a whole. Currently a dance group hires part of the building and brings in a significant amount in letting fees. To address this, "we preach about stewardship and giving but it's not 'do this or we close'. . . . you know I'm pleased with that." The parish as a whole was not as financially sound as he would hope. As an illustration, he said that the London Diocese expects every parish with one priest to pay £85,000 per annum to the Common Fund; St Clement's Parish manages to pay £69,000, so it is in effect being subsidised by other churches in the diocese. In spite of that, it still makes the largest contribution of the 13 churches in its deanery. The stability of Holy Cross is therefore an important issue and the key to Fr Stephen's vision for the future. The founding vision has been maintained and refreshed. Unlike the other two churches in this study, because it has been established longer, Holy Cross is now at the stage of consolidation. Fr Stephen's continuing vision will ensure that this happens.

St Paul's Community Church, Melchester

The vision that established St Paul's was summed up by Fr Sam in these words: "I think we'll want to be a beacon of hope on an estate that sometimes is very hopeless, yes, and I think we can do that by being actually something nice." I have described under the heading of "worship" how Fr Sam set about this.

Since the change of the sponsoring church to All Saints, their vision for St Paul's has come to predominate and that needs putting into context as to how it will affect St Paul's. I summarize Fr Sam's description of it. All Saints is a large charismatic Evangelical church in the centre of Melchester, with a history of church planting and a mainly eclectic middle-class congregation, but with significant work with children and students (Melchester has two large universities). Its three previous plants were in the south of Melchester, which is more prosperous than the north of the city where St Paul's is situated. The model which was approved by the diocesan bishop at that time was that the Vicar of All Saints was appointed as priest-in-charge of the plant in an existing church building and a curate would be responsible for the day-to-day activity. Once the plant was established, the vicar withdrew and the curate was then appointed as priest-in-charge of the new or revived church. The vision of All Saints was to make some impact in the north of the city as "there's not a lot going on in Evangelical circles in the north". It was also the first time that All Saints would be involved with a plant that already had a priest in place and one who did not fully share its style of worship and theology.

However, Fr Sam sees a difference in the vision for St Paul's. "We are trying to do things differently as All Saints has agreed to temporary teams. So, the idea is not that the team will come in and be the new church, but the team is coming in to support the church and put a floor under it. And each member of the team is only committing to a year and All Saints is committing to four years." Fr Sam reminded me that the Bishop's Mission Order is due to be reviewed in four years' time. His "blue sky scenario" is for him to take it through the renewal and turn St Paul's into a church with a legal Church of England basis. The current stage he sees as a transition from its early and quite tenuous start through to being a "real church". The change of sponsorship which has led almost to the imposition of a different vision has been difficult for Fr Sam. It remains to be seen how much he can influence this vision to maintain St Paul's place as a "beacon of hope" and not become a clone of All Saints. It is sad to note that because of the Covid restrictions and the suspension of worship during months of lockdown, much of this vision has come to nought.

Leadership

In his book *Towards a Theology of Church Growth*, David Goodhew writes: "It is worth noting at this point that the earliest churches had established leadership from the beginning."[17] So clear leadership of a church plant should follow this pattern. The role of the founding leader of a church plant can be likened to the way in which the apostles planted

---

17   David Goodhew (ed.), *Towards a Theology of Church Growth* (Farnham: Ashgate, 2015), p. 7.

churches after Pentecost. Paul wrote to the church in Corinth: "I planted, Apollos watered, but God gave the growth."[18] So leadership, and the way in which the leader carries forward and enthuses others about the vision, is as vital for growth and viability of the plant as it is for more established churches.

St Pancras, Rushey Common
It can clearly be seen from the description of this church in the previous chapter that Fr Francis was a key driver behind the way in which St Pancras developed. He had the vision and was allowed by the Vicar of St Paul's to follow it through. Respondent 6 to the questionnaire mentioned "the energy of Fr Francis", and Respondent 9 said that "Fr Francis is doing a terrific job". Yet he himself recognized that the initial leadership of Fr Charles, the Vicar of All Saints, was necessary to get the project off the ground. Once it had been agreed, Fr Francis took over that leadership role and carried it through. Interestingly I found one criticism of what had been done in respect of St Pancras. Respondent 10, an older woman who had been attending St Pancras for over 30 years, complained: "They have neglected our past strengths." Unfortunately, this was not qualified further, and this statement is very much at odds with the view of the Area Bishop and other diocesan officers about the state of the parish in the reports that were prepared concerning the future of the benefice as referred to in an earlier chapter. This outlying comment is also at odds with Fr Francis's view: "when I came here, well people were here already. Yes, I mean I changed things but that doesn't mean that I don't respect the past." There is always this tension when a church plant (or to use the preferred London diocesan word "graft") moves into an existing congregation, especially if that congregation is seen by the diocesan officials to be "weak" or "failing", adjectives often used in such situations, although these adjectives are usually not recognized by those attending these churches. The fact that within a couple of years Fr Francis has achieved so much with the support of so many speaks volumes about the calibre of his leadership. He recognizes also that as leader there are

---

[18] 1 Corinthians 3:6. This model is so important as we see the different roles that are needed. The "planter" may not be the right person to consolidate.

frustrations, especially when things do not move as quickly as he would wish: "I keep telling myself, this is like a plant, yes it is literally a plant. I can water it, put it in the right position for the plant to receive the right amount of sun, avoiding the plant to die, but it's not up to me . . . So, you planted this six months ago. Do I expect it to be a tree now? The church is a bit like this." As a model of collaborative and focussed leadership, the way in which Fr Francis has led St Pancras can be seen as a good example for others in similar situations to follow.

Holy Cross, Greystone
Because Fr Stephen has been involved with Holy Cross since its inception, a specific leadership style around the establishment of a church plant is difficult to discern. In many ways, he fits the stereotypical model of a traditional Anglo-Catholic priest, but his style is not autocratic and I have no evidence that he believes that "Father knows best", which is so often the criticism of Anglo-Catholic clergy and their congregations. He is approachable and pastoral, and his congregation respect this facet of his ministry. Respondent 6, who previously attended a Roman Catholic church, commented: "I feel comfortable here; the priests are lovely." That comfort reflects his calm and pastoral approach to a very racially diverse congregation. This is echoed by Respondent 11, a middle-aged man who formerly attended a Black Evangelical church. He valued "The peace and service programme and detail of the service." These comments from people with very different previous church experiences are testimony to the way in which Fr Stephen leads his church.

St Paul's Community Church, Melchester
Given that this is such a new church plant, with a very small congregation, it is hard to identify a leadership style, as Fr Sam, assisted by his family, does virtually everything, even at times making the tea and coffee whilst his wife runs the craft activity. In his position, he has to make all the decisions and take responsibility for them. He does discuss ideas with the congregation to gain their opinions when a change might be envisaged. So, the planned move to a weekly service, at the time of writing on hold because of Covid-19 restrictions, was discussed at a service. This is how he explained the decision: "But we're moving to weekly. That's the plan;

by the end of this academic year, we want to go weekly. I think I see the sort of fortnightly or monthly doesn't give people enough structure of ownership . . . What we found is that actually we have people come, like all churches, some weeks and not others. In fact, we kind of think that if we went to weekly that wouldn't be an issue." There is no doubt that he is somewhat of a larger-than-life figure. Such a persona works well both in the school and the wider neighbourhood as it takes him away from looking like what many people think a vicar should look like. He feels it makes him more approachable and in the informality of the style of worship, this appears to be so. The role of a pioneer leader can often be a lonely one, especially when change is forced externally. The fact that Fr Sam is coping with this major change in sponsorship and style of the supporting church does show a determined leader.

Growth

It is probably a truism to say that every church wants to grow. Church plants generally are no exception to this and for some, there is an imperative to grow and then reproduce themselves in another place. An example of such a church is St Paul's, Shadwell which between 2010 and 2014 sent out four different groups to plant new congregations in existing churches.[19] Most others have more modest ambitions with a desire to grow to enable them to reach a level of independence from their founding congregation. This is the case with the three churches in this study.

St Pancras, Rushey Common

Fr Francis saw as evidence of growth the change in the nature of the congregation since he became responsible for St Pancras: "The massive change I've seen from the beginning—we went from a very elderly congregation to a young congregation." This had particularly struck me, and this comment was in answer to my observation to him that St Pancras was not a typical Church of England congregation. He also commented that he was frustrated with what he perceived to be the lack of resources to support growth. Two important comments stressed that. "Probably

[19]   Tim Thorlby, *Love, Sweat and Tears* (London: Centre for Theology & Community, 2016), p. 20.

expected more support from the area, the episcopal area. It's always me going to them, saying and provoking them. That's what I am doing . . . So, there are just a few available resources for us when we're doing what I am doing. So, when I look at the Evangelical side, with all due respect, but I see that they throw all the money, a huge amount of resources at them." Later he made a similar comment: "But I see the resources are going somewhere else. When we ask for resources, they are not there for us and also because most of the bishops are not Anglo-Catholics . . . even if they keep repeating that they want to see good Anglo-Catholic mission, it's all on our shoulders." These comments raise serious issues which need addressing if Anglo-Catholic church plants are to flourish, especially in areas where there are large Evangelical churches competing for limited resources. In my experience also, the process for bidding for resources is often quite complex and time-consuming as well as needing some level of technical skill. Fr Francis's message is an important one for deanery and diocesan committees which oversee the allocation of funding for mission initiatives. It must not be down to "the one who shouts loudest" or which has skilled bid writers in the congregation. The other growth point which I have already referred to in this chapter is the Centre for Mindfulness and Spirituality. This Fr Francis sees as a significant initiative and something unique within a Church of England parish. As a result, he has been invited on a number of occasions to address groups of clergy and other church leaders to explain what he is doing in this area. He believes that mindfulness fits well into the Anglo-Catholic tradition of spirituality and the contemplative life. To enable a church plant to grow, maintaining the horticultural metaphor, it needs watering and feeding. It also needs support, not only from its sending church, but from the wider Church of England community around it and its senior diocesan staff.

Holy Cross, Greystone

Fr Stephen, during the time he has been involved, has seen the church grow, but understands that as far as worship is concerned the size of the building is a limitation if more than 60 people were to attend. This I observed on the Patronal Festival in 2019 when 61 people were in attendance, doubtless including some who usually attended St Clement's, as the Bishop of Fulham was celebrating and preaching. The building was uncomfortably crowded. However, given his desire to increase the number of those who see Holy Cross as their church, he sees this as a point of growth. However, he is sceptical of what he sees as happening generally around the church growth agenda, especially in London. He commented: "There is this mindset that HTB has cracked the problem of church growth and if everyone else did the same thing, we'd all be fine." He then described an experience he recently had at a trustees' meeting.[20] "I was at a trustees' meeting at St Mary's, and they were starting to talk about church growth. They said this is what it looks like. What I tried to explain is that it isn't one size fits all. There's no magic trick that if someone bottled and sold it, we'd all be buying it. It is ultimately about stirring up something of God." He was challenged by one of the other trustees who said that they (sc. HTB) must be doing something right as they were opening up a new church. Fr Stephen responded: "the statistics of the last hundred years show that the Church generally is in decline and that's true of all the denominations and that a lot of these new things are just moving Christians around to worship somewhere else". He commented: "and that went down like a plate of cold porridge". This could be said to apply in some measure to Holy Cross as one respondent to the questionnaire said that she had previously attended a Black Evangelical church and another had worshipped in a Roman Catholic church.

Fr Stephen's views on church growth are not unexpected from someone of his tradition. He believes that his church will grow organically by its engagement with its parishioners and by the faithful celebration of the sacraments and the preaching of the word. His rejection of a "one size fits all" model is important as so many churches latch on, probably in desperation, to something that they have seen work well elsewhere, without a proper understanding of the milieu in which it has worked.

St Paul's Community Church, Melchester

Fr Sam had a particular concept of church growth as he saw that the Wednesday school assembly could become a worshipping congregation

---

[20]   Fr Stephen is a trustee of a new church, St Mary's, adjacent to his parish.

that met on Sundays, initially monthly, then fortnightly.[21] He also had a very strong sense of pastoral ministry to his area by building up relationships. He aimed to be visible and ensured that details of church activities were regularly delivered to the flats and houses around. This vision doubtless has been slow to come to fruition, but he believed it was the right one for the area. With the change of sponsorship to All Saints, this concept is being challenged by what he sees as a more aggressive method of evangelism. I have already in this chapter described the tensions between these different approaches. During the time of my visits, I was aware that low numbers were becoming a problem and the fact that this plant did not produce any growth for its original sponsor led that church to divert its funding elsewhere, so putting St Paul's at risk. Fr Sam commented: "As a sustainable model, I'm not sure that Parish Share growth via evangelism is necessarily the appropriate model."[22] On the positive side, he sees the resources that All Saints is providing in terms of the foodbank and the money advice service are a way of introducing people to the church by providing something which shows that the church actually cares about their daily struggles. I finished my research visits just as the change was being put in place. What growth will occur is not yet evidenced and also whether a change of focus will produce the same results in this much more deprived area of Melchester compared with other parts of the city where All Saints has hitherto planted churches.

Sustainability

Given the significant amount of resources, both human and financial, which are devoted to church planting, this is a key area, both for the current activities, and more particularly for the future when the founding planter leaves. I specifically raised this issue with each of the clergy. As far as congregational questionnaire responses were concerned, this did

---

[21]   The change to a Sunday service was intended to free the worship from the physical constraints of a school assembly.

[22]   The Parish Share is the contribution that each parish makes to its diocesan finances to cover the cost of ministry and its support. There are different terminologies to describe this process across the dioceses in the Church of England.

not arise even in a free text answer. This was not surprising as there is a general assumption in churches of all types that the priest, minister or pastor will never leave and so things will continue as they are now. This often proves to be a challenge when it comes to recruiting a successor.

St Pancras, Rushey Common

Fr Francis is convinced that a church plant needs to be "organic and not fake". There is no point in starting well with large numbers of people who come for the novelty and then to find after six months that they have not engaged. For Fr Francis sustainability looks like this: "That's why I think it is very important to centre and to root ourselves in spirituality." As far as the future is concerned, he said: "I frankly don't fear for the future, but I see that the resources are going somewhere else." This is in line with his comments reported in the previous section. I then asked him whether he had a plan for the next five years. His reply was: "yes, stages in order to consolidate our congregation, yes to make it grow, and grow organically, and also to concentrate on the Italian community and the St Pancras Centre for Mindfulness. To consolidate the diversity and also consolidate the space for meditation and contemplation. This spirituality would actually be the root and the heart. I think we are looking five years because I want this to become not dependent on me. It is important that the plant has to become an autonomous entity. I'll still be here because I love it; if I'm not, it will still work, that's very important."

Fr Francis has a clear way forward for the sustainability of St Pancras and a clear plan that has a focus for the continued mission of this church.

Holy Cross, Greystone

Fr Stephen has been in the parish as curate and vicar for the whole of the 11 years of his ordained ministry. He is very realistic about the future. Financially he does not see that Holy Cross would ever be able to pay for a priest, however much it grew; nor could St Clement's afford to contribute to an extra priest. The supply of curates is limited, even more so for "traditionalist" parishes, so there is no guarantee that there always will be a curate in post living in the house attached to Holy Cross; having a curate deprives the parish as a whole of an income of around £15,000 per annum, which they would receive as rent from letting the house, and this needs to be balanced with the availability of additional ministerial support. We discussed what would happen if he were to leave. The parish in living memory had not experienced a vacancy without a priest being available. There had always been a curate to step up to cover. He felt that the weekly Mass would be able to continue as the timing at 5 p.m. meant that there were other priests available. He envisaged some kind of monthly rota to cover this. There were very few retired priests in the area as it was not an area to which people retire. Fr Stephen felt that an imaginative solution would be for a house to be purchased in the area so that an active retired priest could work on a "House for Duty" basis across a number of parishes.[23] He had already made one of the regular worshippers an unofficial churchwarden at Holy Cross, and if he knew that he was leaving, he would identify others to take on leadership roles. Given that Holy Cross is growing to maturity, I believe that it is safe to say that it is now a sustainable congregation, although its finances are still incorporated with those of St Clement's. In an ideal world, the clear separation of the finances would help those who attend Holy Cross to take more responsibility for their future.

St Paul's Community Church, Melchester

This is a much more complex situation, given the change of sponsorship from a small Anglo-Catholic church to that of a large charismatic Evangelical church with a number of years of experience of a particular style of church planting. By the actions of the Archdeacon of Melchester in arranging this transition, it seems likely that the bishop and senior staff want this plant to be sustainable in whatever form that takes. Fr Sam wants to continue up to and through the renewal of the Bishop's Mission Order, after which he feels it will be the right time to hand over to someone else. He was surprised that the bishop at his licensing said: "we need to think about succession". On reflection he thought: "I think it's right in the sense that you need to have a long-term plan which you should allow to change as God wishes." When I spoke to him, he felt he

---

23 House for Duty provides free housing for a retired or self-supporting priest who offers to serve in a parish for an agreed part of the week without payment, other than expenses. It is more common in rural areas.

would be there for another four years or so. Important as Fr Sam is to St Paul's, there is the tension between his vision and the way in which All Saints sees the future.[24] Will they be prepared to go along with Fr Sam's different model, given that they have made a four-year commitment in terms of finance and volunteers, or will they want to replicate what they see as the success of their other plants? The outcome of this will provide significant messages for those from the Anglo-Catholic tradition who want to be church planters.

Conclusion

There is an obvious tension in trying to make generalizable conclusions from the study of three very different churches, but the evidence of the six overlapping themes in these churches does enable some lessons to be drawn which can be applicable in different situations for Anglo-Catholic church planters. Specifically, from the foregoing analysis of the internal themes, there are in addition three external factors of which account needs to be taken. They also have an important influence on whether the plant will be "successful" and also on what the leader of the plant does to work out the vision.

The first is *intentionality*. By this I mean that church planting has to be undertaken positively and as part of a parish, or wider church, strategy. There is a danger that parishes and clergy can be carried away on the latest wave of enthusiasm or by the newest upbeat report and think that a church plant or some other such initiative is the panacea for all their missional failings and so will prove that the mission of that particular church is moving forward. This is the road to failure. It reflects what Jesus was referring to in the Parable of the Sower about the seed which "sprang up quickly, since they had no depth of soil. But when the sun rose, they were scorched; and since they had no root, they withered away."[25] Intentionality gives that depth, that rootedness, as proper preparations have been made, an analysis of the factors for and against undertaking

---

24 This was before Fr Sam's decision to resign.

25 Matthew 13:5–6.

a plant has been carefully undertaken and there is a wide range of acceptance and active support from all the different stakeholders.

The second factor that is essential is the wholehearted support of "the sending church". As an example, I have noted the way in which Fr Francis engaged with the congregation of St Paul's to show them the vision that he had for St Pancras. It was a regular, slow but consistent process and followed the proposal of the Area Bishop to link St Pancras with St Paul's.

In contrast, although St Paul's Community Church had support, in the form of expenses for Fr Sam, I observed very little other support. Other than when the Bishop's Mission Order was delivered and Fr Sam licensed under it, there was only one occasion when I met someone from the "sending church" at a service at St Paul's. When they decided to end the payment of Fr Sam's expenses, Fr Sam commented:

> The parish didn't want to break the link, but they didn't want to resource it. . . . If you've got a parish that is needy, needy is perhaps the wrong word, but a parish that is in need trying to plant a church . . . This is a parish that liked the idea of having somebody there.

Without clear and unqualified support for a guaranteed period of time, there is significant risk that the plant will not survive. The London plants (from a different churchmanship) described by Tim Thorlby in *Love, Sweat and Tears* came with a time-limited "dowry" of both financial and human resources from the sending church.[26] This is similar to what All Saints is now providing for the next four years to support St Paul's.

In the case of Holy Cross, given that it was using a building owned by the parish, and had a curate and a retired priest from St Clement's, as well as a parish priest, as its ministerial support, this was not a significant issue and there was an overlap of congregations—certainly in the earlier stages, and still continuing to some extent.

The third factor is the support *from the wider church and the diocese*. I have noted above that for St Pancras, the planned link with St Paul's was at the instigation of the Area Bishop and was enthusiastically received.

---

26   Thorlby, *Love, Sweat and Tears*.

However, Fr Francis expressed his disappointment at the difficulty he has in obtaining resources. He felt that he was always in competition with the large Evangelical churches in the episcopal area and that there was no real recognition of his need for support. It is perhaps significant that for the whole time that I was attending St Pancras, there was no mention of a visit from a bishop. There does need to be a clear and equitable process for allocating resources, which in Fr Francis's view was not in place.

In contrast, the Bishop of Fulham came to Holy Cross on a number of occasions and Fr Stephen was very appreciative of his pastoral support.[27] The network of traditionalist parishes is a close-knit one and provides mutual support, but Fr Stephen is also actively involved in the life of his non-traditionalist deanery, and is also a trustee of a new church on the borders of his parish.[28]

St Paul's Community Church had the support of the diocese of Melchester from the beginning as it recognized the need of that area, which had been without an obvious Church of England presence since the closure of the medieval church. What seemed to be lacking, in my view, was some underpinning personal support for Fr Sam, other than his attachment to the sponsoring parish and the normal relationship with the area dean and archdeacon. Pioneer ministry can be very lonely and at times depressing. In my experience of involvement in a couple of new churches, one dating back to the late 1970s, there does need to be either a formal or informal support group, a safe place for the priest to sound out ideas and air frustrations and receive encouragement and support. It is possible that the lack of such support indirectly led to the withdrawal of funding by the sponsoring parish.

In this chapter, I have identified the key elements from my research that are important in the support of a church plant, its leader and its congregation from its inception and into its period of consolidation. I

---

[27] Out of the 413 parishes in the Diocese of London, the Bishop of Fulham only has oversight of 46, so he is able to be much more available than the other Area Bishops.

[28] Traditionalist churches are linked through membership of "The Society under the patronage of Saint Wilfrid and Saint Hilda", see <https://www.sswsh.com/diocese-detail.php?id=130>, accessed 24 January 2023.

have evidenced them with verbatim quotations both from interviews and questionnaire responses, thereby ensuring that the lived experiences of those involved are heard, rather than relying on church planting theory. None of these elements are specific to Anglo-Catholics although the emphasis on worship as well as the incarnational style of ministry and mission may not be so strong in other parts of the Church of England. There is therefore no compelling reason, other than in terms of resources, why Anglo-Catholic parishes should not be planting churches. In the next chapter, I will look at these themes in relation to the work of the Victorian Anglo-Catholics, and consider whether the themes can be seen in their activities, as well as any other themes which could be relevant today.

6

Comparisons—then and now

Introduction

This chapter aims to link the Victorian Anglo-Catholic establishment of new churches by two particular individuals, Fr Richard Temple West and Richard Foster, with a description of three present-day church plants that have come out of the Anglo-Catholic tradition. The chapter shows that there are some similarities in approach although the contexts are very different. From my participant observation and the relevant literature, with the help of a thematic analysis (a way of analysing information derived either from personal interviews or questionnaires), I have identified six themes which will be the basis of my comparison.

When we are considering the development of the Oxford Movement, we need to put it into its historical context. 1848 was a tumultuous year across Europe with revolutions or attempted revolutions occurring in France, Italy, the Austro-Hungarian Empire as well as other countries or provinces. In England, there was concern about these events. The Church of England, as the "Established Church", was seen, especially by the middle classes, as a stabilizing element of social control (I have referred in an earlier chapter to the verse from Mrs C. F. Alexander's hymn "All things bright and beautiful" which describes what she believed to be the God-ordained social order of Victorian society). Any change in the Church could be perceived as upsetting this balance. The inclusion of non-Anglicans in Parliament and in other institutions added to this concern; so many felt that the Church was under threat. Although those who originated (if such a word is adequate to describe the issue of Ninety Tracts and their subsequent effects) the "Oxford Movement" thought that they were protesting against constitutional reforms which they saw as endangering the Church and therefore protecting its status against an interfering government, others, like Bishop Bagot, saw the Tracts as a danger to the Church. Anything which might upset the *status quo* whether in doctrine or liturgical practice was to be resisted.

Demography

When considering these two differing periods it is important to see what changes made the Victorians engage in such a widespread programme of church building, especially in urban areas. One of the major differences between the two periods is population change. As an example, which is replicated in many other urban or suburban areas across England, Julian Litten relates how Walthamstow, the main area of Richard Foster's labours, grew from a population of 3,006 to one of 96,720 between 1801 and 1901.[1] He attributes much of this to the period after 1870 when the railway line was opened from Liverpool Street to Chingford, which encouraged housing development and commuting. The single twelfth-century parish church was no longer able to meet the needs of this expanding suburb, so other churches were built, as recounted previously. The same pattern was happening elsewhere in London. John Wolffe of the Open University describes the building of four churches in Finchley between the 1840s and 1890s.[2]

The area of Paddington where Richard Temple West built St Mary Magdalene was already an area of poor housing and even 50 years later, Charles Booth described the deprivation and immorality of the area.[3] But the more wealthy residents who attended All Saints, Margaret Street in the 1850s found the three-mile journey quite challenging, and wanted a

---

[1]   Julian W. S. Litten, *St Barnabas and St James the Greater* (Walthamstow: The PCC of St Barnabas and St James the Greater, 2003), p. 4.

[2]   John Wolffe, "The Chicken or The Egg? Building Anglican Churches and Building Congregations in a Victorian London Suburb", *Material Religion* 9:1 (2013), pp. 36–59.

[3]   Charles Booth, *Life and Labour of the People in London: Third Series: Religious Influences, Volume 3* (London: MacMillan & Co. Ltd, 1902), p. 146.

church nearer to where they lived.[4] The location was probably secondary and depended very much on the availability of a site in an area where, because of recent house-building, empty sites were hard to find.

The initiative for church plants today comes from a similar demographic concern. In some places, as in my own parish, it was driven as a response to the need for a Christian presence in a new housing area. In others, a new church is planted in an existing area where the visible Christian presence has become weak or has disappeared. The data from the research supports this contention.

The witness of St Pancras, Rushey Common was seen by the diocesan authorities to be very weak and had been making little impact in its parish for a number of years. When it fell vacant, the opportunity was taken to find a way of reviving it; if that failed, it would be closed. A church plant/graft was proposed by the diocesan authorities and initiated with the support of St Paul's. Active Christian witness became obvious at the church, with the help of large banners on the external wall opposite the park and the bus stop, and the open doors, as well as Fr Francis's large email contact list.

In the case of Holy Cross, Greystone, the parish church was situated at the extreme northern boundary of the parish and was invisible to most of the parish. The Mission Hall, in the south of the parish, had been out of use as far as the church was concerned for nearly 70 years. The area of the parish in which it was situated was somewhat more ethnically diverse than the northern part of the parish. The missional imperative was to establish a centre of Christian witness and worship in that part of the parish. That was done by starting a Sunday afternoon Mass and advertising it both with leaflets and by the use of a large "A-board" placed strategically outside in the middle of the pavement. This encouraged some local people to attend, especially older people whose mobility was limited, as public transport to the parish church was very inconvenient and involved a walk of several hundred metres at the end of the bus journey. This represents an example of a virtually disused church-owned

---

[4]   T. T. Carter, *Richard Temple West—A Record of Life and Work* (London: J. Masters & Co., 1895), p. 33.

building being brought back into use in an unchurched area so as to provide a physical Christian presence in an area previously devoid of one.

For St Paul's Community Church in Melchester, there is a somewhat similar situation in respect of the lack of a visible and viable Christian presence. The medieval Grade II-listed building had not been used for worship since its closure in 2010 under the auspices of the then Archdeacon of Leicester, who has since become my Suffragan Bishop when a decision was taken to close it based on the dwindling numbers of regular worshippers. Since then, it has slowly been falling into disrepair and had been subjected to sporadic vandalism and break-ins. What did exist was a church school named after the closed parish church, but until the arrival of Fr Sam and the establishment of St Paul's Community Church, the Christian presence was purely nominal. With the opening of St Paul's Community Church there was once more a place of worship in what previously was a relatively unchurched area.

These three contemporary examples demonstrate the way in which one of the drivers for Victorian church building has been translated into present-day situations to ensure a wider and more visible Christian presence in these areas. Demographic and geographical considerations very often underpin current church planting, as individual churches and wider church organizations endeavour to meet the needs of a changing population.

Philanthropy and funding

Perhaps the greatest difference between the setting up of new churches in Victorian times and in the present day is the way in which they are funded. Sarah Flew has documented in great detail the philanthropic activities that funded much of church life in London in the second half of the nineteenth century and into the Edwardian era up to the beginning of the First World War.[5] But with the passing of time, the large church-building

---

[5]   Sarah Flew, *Philanthropy and the Funding of the Church of England, 1856–1914* (London: Pickering & Chatto, 2015). It was at the end of this period that St Pancras was built.

funds, to which philanthropists and corporations contributed, have in the main ceased to exist. Any funding available is now usually allocated by the Church Commissioners to dioceses for the support of projects in parishes. It is not usually large-scale capital funding. I have related in an earlier chapter the very extensive philanthropic giving by Richard Foster to enable new churches. Similarly, I have noted the way in which Richard Temple West was able to accumulate funding towards his various projects. His biographer, T. T. Carter, commented:

> It was afterwards said of West, by the Archbishop's secretary, that he was the best beggar in London, that he could collect for charitable purposes £5,000 a year through his offertories. We can understand what would have been his efforts for a church of his own.[6]

On the following page, Carter records how, when it was decided to build an aisle to enlarge the church, "two ladies sold their house and furniture, which just met the required sum".[7] Documents stored at the London Metropolitan Archive show that West provided a very detailed half-yearly statement of the finances of St Mary Magdalene for his congregation, accompanied by an exhortation to maintain or increase giving in order to support and extend the ministry of the church.[8]

None of the three plants in my research had any real initial financial backing. St Pancras was supported on a day-to-day basis by St Paul's, but with the intention that it should eventually become financially independent. Holy Cross still does not have its finances separate from those of St Clement's. St Paul's Community Church did receive an annual grant of £4,000 from its sponsoring church for running expenses, but that was withdrawn after only two years and the money diverted to employing a children and family's worker, based at the parish church. This led to the change of sponsoring church, to one which agreed to maintain that

---

[6]   Carter, *Temple West*, p. 34.

[7]   Carter, *Temple West*, p. 35.

[8]   Evidenced from personal access to uncatalogued material on 4 June 2021.

amount for four years. The Diocese of Melchester supplied the vicar's stipend and housing as part of its support of pioneer ministry.

However, in the wider world of church planting, there is a significant difference. St Paul's, Shadwell in east London was one of the first plants in that area supported by Holy Trinity, Brompton. Tim Thorlby relates:

> [There was] a grant of £50,000 from HTB, to be drawn down as required, plus a further goodwill offering of c. £35,000 (including Gift Aid) collected from the wider HTB Network at Focus, their annual summer gathering.[9]

There was a "founding dowry" or "seed corn" in excess of £80,000 with the expectation that St Paul's would become self-supporting. This was soon to be the case as St Paul's later went on to plant a congregation in St Peter's, Bethnal Green and gave a start-up "goodwill gift of £10,000".[10] Similarly, when St Paul's initiated a church plant in All Hallows, Bow, St Paul's provided over £160,000 to All Hallows over five years.[11] Such large amounts of financial support are beyond the wildest dreams of present day Anglo-Catholic churches who wish to instigate a church plant as there are no comparable large and wealthy churches willing to support such a range of church plants. Instead, they are left to the vagaries and uncertainties of bidding for diocesan project funding, provided by the Church Commissioners.

Intentionality

In my view, this was as important to the Victorian church builders as it is today for those who wish to engage in church planting. From my reading of the biographies of Richard Temple West and Richard Foster, described in a previous chapter, it can be seen that these men were very

---

9   Tim Thorlby, *Love, Sweat and Tears* (London: Centre for Theology & Community, 2016), p. 21.

10 Thorlby, *Love, Sweat and Tears*, p. 45.

11 Thorlby, *Love, Sweat and Tears*, p. 60.

much focussed on and driven by their projects. West devoted himself to the establishment and ongoing support of St Mary Magdalene, even after a disastrous fire before the building was completed. Within a couple of hours of the fire being extinguished, he had posted placards on the still-hot church walls announcing ten services on the following day in the chapel of St Ambrose, the "tin tabernacle" that preceded the building of St Mary Magdalene, to thank God that the damage had been limited. The first service of Holy Communion was scheduled for 4 a.m.[12] The fire is described in very great detail by William Scott, one of West's curates, who carefully documented his ministry.[13]

Foster had a similar enthusiasm. In his diary he observed that his interest in church growth preceded 1848. He had tried without success to persuade the people of West Hackney parish, which he had been attending for ten years, to extend the church to provide more free seats for the poor.[14] He failed in this attempt.[15] But in 1848 he joined with others in forming a committee to promote the building of the church of St Matthias and an adjacent school for an area of Stoke Newington and Hornsey which had 5,000 inhabitants and no local church. He was the honorary secretary to the committee. The school opened on All Saints' Day 1849 and was used for worship until the church was consecrated on 13 June 1853. His biographer writes:

> He [Foster] always looked on it as the beginning of his endeavours towards improving the spiritual and physical conditions of thousands in the poorest parts of London.[16]

---

[12] Carter, *Temple West*, pp. 36–7.

[13] William Scott, *Fifty Years at St Mary Magdalene, Paddington* (London: H. G. Saunders & Son, 1918).

[14] Most churches in the first half of the nineteenth century had box pews which were rented out. The poor had some benches on which they could sit; otherwise, they would have to stand. So "the weakest went to the wall" as the saying goes.

[15] W. F. Foster, *Richard Foster* (London: Eyre & Spottiswood Ltd., 1914 (private circulation)), p. 45.

[16] Foster, *Richard Foster*, pp. 52–3.

These examples show clearly the drive and the energy which these two men possessed and which enabled them to carry out the work to which they believed that they had been called by God.

In the previous chapter, six themes were described which had been identified from my research. These themes now need to be considered in relation to the work that West and Foster undertook to see whether they are mirrored in part or in whole in their work, taking into consideration the different historical contexts.

Worship

For West, as a priest, the conduct of worship in his church was obviously a significant priority, and as an Anglo-Catholic, he would wish it to be of a high standard in every respect. It is fortunate that his biographer was able to have access to a contemporary account of a weekday evensong in St Mary Magdalene at the beginning of Advent 1872. The chronicler starts his account as follows:

> A great deal has been said of late years respecting the various merits of High and Low Church worship. I therefore determined to judge for myself, and chose for my *locale* S. Mary Magdalene's, of which the Rev. R. T. West is the Vicar.[17]

The writer describes the atmosphere before the service started and comments approvingly that the sexes were seated separately and commends this practice to others. He then goes through the service noting significant points. He was very impressed by the congregational singing both of the psalms and the hymns. He said that the extempore sermon, preached by West, "was, as far as I understand the word, Evangelical".[18] He finishes his report with these words:

---

[17]   Carter, *Temple West*, p. 39.

[18]   Carter, *Temple West*, p. 40. This comment refers to the content of the sermon rather than any style of worship. Often there was little to distinguish in

The whole service seemed throughout to be marked by deep reverence, and the congregation seemed impressed with the thought of Whose Presence was among them. There was a slight inclination of the head at the *Gloria Patri*, and at the name of JESUS, otherwise I saw nothing extraordinary. My advice to those who have never been to a High Church service is to go and see, if they can discern any want of reverence, or anything likely to take their thoughts from the holy purpose for which they are met together.[19]

Another writer had visited St Mary Magdalene on Easter Day 1872. He was impressed both by the numbers attending and the style of worship. This is the conclusion of his article:

> [O]n returning home, one could not but feel after such a service as that, at S. Mary Magdalene's, that there is life in the old Church yet. It is no question about niceties of doctrine or the fashion of a vestment. It is a question of life and death.[20]

A third writer was impressed by the reverence of the congregation which he attributed to the influence of West over his parishioners. He also commented on the number of young men who were present.

West was keen to defend, but not aggressively, what he believed to be the essentials of Anglo-Catholic worship; a writer of a letter to the *West London Express* on 27 April 1878 noted these as "the daily Eucharist, lights, vestments, and the Eastward position".[21] Worship, conducted as in the apostolic injunction "decently and in order", was the centre around which West built his ministry.[22]

---

content between Evangelical and Anglo-Catholic sermons, although the need for repentance and "turning to Christ" were paramount in the former.

19 Carter, *Temple West*, p. 41.
20 Carter, *Temple West*, p. 42.
21 Carter, *Temple West*, p. 45.
22 1 Corinthians 14:40.

As far as Richard Foster is concerned there is less evidence of his attitude to the style of worship. Litten describes him as a keen supporter of the Oxford Movement although Foster referred to himself as a "Prayer Book Churchman".[23] He was a regular worshipper and every day after breakfast would attend Morning Prayer at West Hackney Parish Church before walking to his office in the City. Yet, despite his devotion to this service, he was very aware of the limitations of the standard Prayer Book services. His son wrote: "The clergy, out of touch with their parishioners, were holding services in such a way which made no appeal to men's [sic] hearts".[24] Foster was impressed by the different style of worship at Leeds Parish Church, conducted by Walter Hook, one of the prominent men in the Oxford Movement. His son reflected his views:

> Instead of the lifeless service he was accustomed to in London of the old three-decker type, carried on between parson and clerk in a bare church, with little singing, and that mostly bad, little congregational worship, with long dull sermons, preached by a clergyman in a long black gown to a small somnolent congregation, he found for the first time a surpliced choir, a service bright and congregational, preaching good and bracing, the church beautifully decorated, and, in consequence, a large and enthusiastic congregation.[25]

This experience led Foster to the belief that different types of services were necessary for different congregations—a revolutionary idea at the time which, over a century and a half later, would indeed fit in with the ideas proposed in *Mission-Shaped Church*. In his correspondence, there are numerous letters which emphasize the same point: "we want short, fervid services with arousing, energetic sermons which would come home to the thoughts and feelings of the poor".[26]

---

23 Litten, *St Barnabas and St James the Greater*, p. 5.

24 Foster, *Richard Foster*, p. 60.

25 Foster, *Richard Foster*, p. 60.

26 Foster, *Richard Foster*, p. 63.

It can be seen therefore that just as "worship" is a key theme for the present-day church plants and the main public and obvious focus of their activities, it was equally important to the Victorians. The offering of reverent, accessible and well-executed worship was and still is seen as an important way of attracting worshippers into the churches as well as underpinning the other activities of a church. Many current advertisements for church services stress their style of worship, using such words as "lively", "relevant", "reverent", or "inclusive", to name but a few. Job adverts for clergy often include similar phrases. The physical activity of worship is vital but is not a "one size fits all" to meet the needs of everyone; one person's preference for worship songs with guitars, drums and lighting effects is anathema for those who want what they see as traditional worship, and vice versa.

In their own spheres of influence, both West and Foster worked to ensure that this was happening. For West, it was evidenced in the size of his congregations, such as 1,122 communicants on Easter Day 1872. Foster used his wealth to support "those who, so long as they were orthodox, filled their churches, although their services might be more ritualistic than he himself cared for".[27]

Community

The concept of a "church community" or a "church family", which is seen to be so important today in the majority of churches, was probably unknown to the Victorian Anglo-Catholics who looked rather at the role of the church in relation to its parish. An extensive search of literature fails to find any reference to this concept, as it would be understood today. Neither do either of my major sources, the biographies of Richard Temple West and Richard Foster, mention anything which could be aligned with this. In this respect, we cannot learn anything from their experience. Their concept of community was outward-facing and seen as the way in which the Church, both locally and nationally, engaged with the wider society, particularly in the absence of organized state health, welfare and

---

[27]   Foster, *Richard Foster*, p. 64.

educational provision, such as Social Services, state-maintained schools or the National Health Service.

West certainly saw his ministry in this light. Not content with having established St Mary Magdalene as a place of worship, he set up a great range of agencies to support the less fortunate members of society. For his own church he set up a choir school, but alongside this, he founded private schools for different classes. He established a home for religious sisters who worked in his parish, a penitentiary home, a working men's club, a nurses' institute which trained and supported nurses. He founded a daughter church, St Martha's, "intended for a simpler worship to suit those for whom choral singing was a difficulty".[28] Outside of the parish were a female prisoners' hostel for those ending their sentences and a Sanatorium for Inebriates in Spelthorne, about 16 miles away from Paddington. All of these were personally supported by West. Carter reports the Bishop of Nassau, a contemporary, friend, and supporter of West, saying that it was "about the most notable organization for home missionary purposes that had been seen in an English town parish in modern times".[29] Such was the impact of West on his parish and the wider community. This is confirmed in his obituary in the *Church Times*, which lists some of these impacts.[30]

Foster's contribution to the community and the mission of the Church can be seen in his philanthropic activities in supporting the building of new churches. But his concern went beyond the spiritual to the physical needs of people. He involved himself in school boards as "the supremacy of the Church was threatened by the Dissenters".[31] He was treasurer of the London Hospital and a governor of St Bartholomew's Hospital. He built houses in Walthamstow and took an interest in their gardens to the extent that he employed a gardener to look after them. He founded a society in 1857 to improve cottages in the older part of Hastings as well as setting up in 1861 the London Labourers' Dwellings Society to

---

28   Foster, *Richard Foster*, p. 44.

29   Carter, *Temple West*, p. 44.

30   *Church Times*, 17 February 1893, p. 168.

31   Foster, *Richard Foster*, p. 134.

support improvements in housing in the poorer parts of London.[32] Ahead of his time, he also supported co-partnership in the South Metropolitan Gas Company in which he was a major shareholder. In addition to all of these, he supported what would now be described as environmental activities as he was keen to subscribe to the preservation of green open spaces in north London.

Both of these men embraced the idea of community as being an integral part both of the mission of the Church and of the lives of Christians as individuals. Like the three research churches, they were determined that the gospel should be lived out and witnessed to in the wider communities, the parishes, in which they were involved. A strong response to the needs of the community, beyond the walls of the church, is a factor which can contribute to the success of a church plant.

Vision

The concept of vision in a formal sense is a relatively modern idea and is an important part of the business world, in which companies draw up their vision for the future to show how they see themselves developing. This is also designed to draw attention to the company and make it stand out against its competitors. Many churches today have adopted this practice and have devised short statements which summarize their vision. The Church of England website has a section devoted to helping churches articulate their visions.[33] West and Foster certainly would not have had "a vision statement", but the way in which they worked showed that each of them had a clear vision for their activities. Each of them knew the type of church they were establishing. West was keen to replicate the style of worship at All Saints, Margaret Street. Foster's building of St Barnabas, Walthamstow was designed for Anglo-Catholic worship. (It maintains these features today with the altar set for the *ad*

---

orientem celebration of the Eucharist and a tabernacle for the Reserved Sacrament on the shelf behind, with six very tall candlesticks.) But these were individual and personal visions rather than dictated or imposed by a diocesan strategy—let alone one which was policed by the archdeacon or a committee, through an audit of each parish's Mission Action Plans. There would not have been any sense of it being replicated in the same way in other areas or parishes.

When the idea of establishing a mission in Paddington was raised, West was asked to carry it out. He enthusiastically responded and made that vision his own. With the help of one of the Paddington residents, a Mr D. Wood, who eventually became a key figure at St Mary Magdalene's, he spent every Saturday afternoon exploring various parts of Paddington to find a site for this new church. When he found the site, he immediately began the work of building the church. In fact, he started with a temporary church, which was known as the chapel of St Ambrose. The way in which this church was organized was reported in one of the journals of the day:

> The arrangement of the Sunday Services is somewhat novel, and it will be curious to see whether the plan answers. They are as follows: Holy Communion, 8 a.m.; Morning Prayer and Sermon, 10; Holy Communion, 10.30; Litany, 3; First Evensong 3.30; Second Evensong and Sermon, 7.[34]

£2,200 had already been subscribed towards the purchase of the site, and West sought to raise a further £2,600 to underpin the building of a permanent church and its associated school. The vision of others that he had made his own was becoming so successful that the plan to have a clergy house built adjacent to the church, which was a common feature of Victorian churches, was abandoned in favour of increasing the size of the church by building an aisle. Throughout his ministry West maintained the vision that was behind the foundation of St Mary Magdalene.

Foster had seen the need for new or extended churches well before 1848 as he had tried to persuade West Hackney Parish Church to expand. Unfortunately, he failed in this. But in 1848 he met a number of men who

---

[34]   Carter, *Temple West*, pp. 33–4.

wanted to build a district church for Stoke Newington and Hornsey.[35] This proved to be the beginning of a long association and the founding in 1854 of what might be described as a fraternity—the Stoke Newington and Hackney Church Association. It had a clear vision which describes exactly Foster's own views. Rule II states:

> That the object of the Association be the Glory of God in the extension of His Church by all lawful means, the promotion of the increase and efficient performance of all the Offices of the Church, the diffusion of Christian knowledge, the exercise of Works of Charity, and the Mutual Improvement of the Members of the Association.[36]

The rules go on to explain how these objects are to be fulfilled and it can be seen from them that they were an important influence on Foster's life. For his vision was not only about physically building new churches and extending older ones; there was a serious spiritual side with a focus on mission as the association expected its members "to embrace the opportunities it affords of helping the sick and needy, instructing the ignorant, reclaiming the wanderers and outcasts, and sending the blessed Gospel to the Heathen".[37] For both of these men, there was a clear vision of what they wanted to achieve. Like their twenty-first century counterparts, they had a desire to share the good news of Jesus Christ in word and deed in areas of need and consistently worked towards this end.

Leadership

From the previous sections, it can be seen that both West and Foster were outstanding leaders. They knew what they wanted to achieve and were able to encourage others to follow them in doing so. Once West had accepted the vision of the Paddington Mission, he devoted all his

---

[35] Foster, *Richard Foster*, pp. 51–2.

[36] Foster, *Richard Foster*, p. 56.

[37] Foster *Richard Foster*, p. 57.

energies to it. From what is recorded by Carter in West's biography, this was crucial in ensuring that the church succeeded. From the service records in the London Metropolitan Archive, it can be seen that West led a team of a number (usually around six) of other clergy, who shared with him in the conduct of worship. From the biography it is clear that throughout his ministry, West led his church in a very obvious and gifted way. A journal at the time remarked: "It is evident that neither Mr. West, nor his parishioners are disposed to let the grass grow under their feet."[38] Similarly another journal commented: "It says much for Mr. West's influence over people and administrative capacity that he had formed what I hear is considered a model congregation."[39]

Foster also showed significant leadership. The Stoke Newington and Hackney Church Association has already been mentioned, but he took a leading role in ensuring that new parishes were established across north London as well as supporting the Bishop of Rochester's scheme for new churches in south London, the Ten Churches Scheme. His support was to such an extent that not only was he a leading member of the committee, but also he contributed financially to setting up two mission districts, paying for two clergy and contributing to the purchase of the sites for these churches.[40] He also was instrumental in promoting the quite revolutionary idea at that time of "associated parishes—rich and poor". The aim was that a rich parish would link with a poor parish to support it both in terms of finance and workers.[41] The link between Chislehurst, where he lived after moving from Clapton, and St Katherine's, Rotherhithe was one to which he gave significant support and energy. These two men showed in their differing ways significant leadership in the areas of church work with which they were involved. The success of St Mary Magdalene and the various projects which occupied Foster are evidence of this.

---

[38] Carter, *Temple West*, p. 39.

[39] Carter, *Temple West*, p. 44.

[40] Foster, *Richard Foster*, pp. 126–7.

[41] This has only come to be an accepted way of support over the last 30 years or so through the work of the Church Urban Fund.

This type of leadership was very different from that which is frequently referred to today in Church Growth and Church Planting literature.[42] As seen above, leadership as a concept was unchallenged in the Victorian Church. It was the role of the parson in each parish with no contention, except perhaps from a patron who might want to exert pressure for the parson to conform to his expectations, political or social. The current concept of "lay leaders" or "shared leadership" within an individual congregation, or a lay-led church, would be outside the Victorian experience and probably comprehension. The engaged laity, often middle class and relatively wealthy, supported the clergy in their view of what the church should be doing as well as providing funding. Lay people were involved in ministry, such as "parish visitors" or "scripture readers", but these were supportive, not leadership, roles. Foster accepted this view although he was unwilling to support "lazy clergy"; he donated to causes which he felt he could support and was heavily involved as a layman in much of church activity, as has been noted in earlier chapters.

Growth

The concern with church growth which so preoccupies the Church of England today would have been alien both to West and Foster. What would have been more familiar would have been ensuring that churches met the needs of those who lived in the parish. Churches were built to meet the needs of a given and usually growing area. The seats available and the size of the worship space were planned according to the population of the area to be served. So new churches were built in areas of new housing to meet the needs of a growing population, especially in large cities. The main motive was evangelism, to reach the unchurched, but there was also the fear of competition from other denominations as well as the underlying desire to maintain some form of social control. In Leeds, Walter Hook (who has already been mentioned in connection

---

[42] Mission and Public Affairs Council, *Mission-Shaped Church: Church Planting and Fresh Expressions of Church in a Changing Context* (London: Church House Publishing, 2004), passim.

with both West and Foster) undertook considerable work to ensure that there were sufficient Anglican churches and clergy to meet the needs of that fast-growing city, especially as Methodism had become the largest denomination following John Wesley's visit in July 1764.[43]

As I have commented, this modern concept of "church growth", so evident in much of the literature as well as in diocesan strategies, would not have been understood in the Victorian age. Churches were built and few, if any, from my research, were closed. In my diocese, when I was a member of the "Closed Churches Uses Committee", we had two sites; one was a crumbling roofless sixteenth-century building, miles away from any habitation in a copse on top of a hill, and the other a derelict tower. These were still theoretically open for worship because the legal processes for closure had never been implemented. Because they had not legally been closed, at the very least they needed to be insured, thus being a drain on resources available for the present-day church.

As has been noted earlier, West saw this not only through worship, although the 1,122 communicants on Easter Day 1872 testify to the fact that the worship that was offered met the spiritual needs of those who attended.[44] He also ensured that the physical needs of his parishioners were met by the range of social and community projects described earlier. However, Charles Booth at the end of the nineteenth century wryly commented:

> The elaborate services at St. Mary Magdalene's draw good congregations but not to any extent from parishioners; nor do any large number attend the special mission services. The clergy are devoted to their work, and the people, they say, are full of gratitude, respect and love; 'there is no unwillingness to come to church'—*only they do not come*.[45]

---

[43]   <https://covenant.livingchurch.org/2021/12/15/the-greatest-anglo-catholic-church-planter/>, accessed 24 January 2023.

[44]   Carter, *Temple West*, p. 41.

[45]   Booth, *Life and Labour*, Vol. 3, p. 120 (my italics).

Foster was concerned not only by the lack of churches in some areas but also that,

> in London the want of churches and clergy was not so serious a feature of the situation as the fact that the existing churches, overcrowded as they should have been, were far from full.[46]

This comment shows Foster's concern that the church of his time was losing its appeal, especially among the "lower classes", because of its unwillingness to adapt and meet the needs of the wider population. He was looking for more attractive worship. As his biographer wrote:

> ... the times required other methods. [This] taught him that there was no fixed rule as to what type of service was right, and that in different times and with different congregations a different degree of ritual might be desirable.[47]

Even though our modern concept of church growth was unknown to West and Foster, the underlying desire to have a flourishing and well-attended church was a key issue for them. They saw it as a sign that the Church was fulfilling its mission of bringing the Christian faith to the whole of society.

Sustainability

If "growth" were a somewhat alien concept to West and Foster, that of "sustainability" would seem to be even more so. Like the thousands of medieval churches which were open for worship, any new church would just increase the accessibility of a place of worship in a given area. Each new church needs to establish a structure that can ensure that it can continue, even after the founding planter relinquishes responsibility for its support. This is important today as every church, new and old, has

---

[46] Foster, *Richard Foster*, p. 60.

[47] Ibid., p. 61.

to look towards its future in terms of ministry and financial resources. The Victorian Church did not have such bodies as Diocesan Boards of Finance or Boards of Ministry to oversee this. The previous section on Philanthropy goes some way to explaining how churches were financed as well as mentioning the existence of various episcopally supported building funds and committees, which generally no longer exist. It is therefore difficult to link the Victorian Church with this modern concept because of the vast difference in culture within church and society as well as the changes in the structure and financing of the Church of England over the intervening years. In all my historical reading, I have found nothing to suggest that the Victorians regarded their new churches as being anything other than permanent and enduring, like the many thousands of medieval churches that had been ministering to parishes, large and small, throughout England for centuries; the new churches were seen as additions to fill in the gaps that the changes in population had brought about, hence the large church-building programme in Walthamstow. This was repeated across England. In my own parish, a mission church was built in 1865 to meet a growing, relatively small, housing area and demolished in 1969 because it was unsafe and sparsely attended.[48] In many other places, Victorian churches have been demolished, or have become centres of worship for other denominations or faith communities, or changed for secular uses.

Conclusion

This chapter brings into contrast the labours of the Victorians and what is happening today. It shows that most of the factors that should promote current Anglo-Catholic church planting were present in the ways that Richard Temple West and Richard Foster were working for church building and expansion in the mid-nineteenth century. There are caveats, as the social, demographic and ecclesiastical situations are not in any

---

[48] <https://bedsarchives.bedford.gov.uk/CommunityHistories/ LeightonBuzzard/SaintAndrewsChurchLeightonBuzzard.aspx>, accessed 24 January 2023.

way comparable. For example, attending church today is not the mark of social respectability as it was among certain classes in the Victorian era, nor is there the equivalent in rural parishes of pressure from "the squire or landlord" to attend church. For those who want to attend church, particularly in large cities and towns, there is much more variety on offer as well as it being much easier to attend a preferred church even at a considerable distance from your home. Contrast this ease of travel with one of the reasons for West building St Mary Magdalene's—to avoid those who attended All Saints, Margaret Street and lived in west London having to travel slowly and with difficulty across London. Yet there is a strong common thread that runs through the way in which churches have been planted or built to meet the specific needs of different areas. Without a vision for growth and a committed and supported leadership, new Victorian churches and current church plants would not have been established. So, as has been demonstrated above, the Victorian pioneers and our modern leaders of church plants have much in common in the ways that they have worked to establish a Christian presence for the spread of the gospel.

Conclusion

This book has covered a wide field of study in an Anglo-Catholic context, from describing the ministry of a mid-Victorian cleric and that of an Anglo-Catholic merchant who was a very generous philanthropist, to three very ordinary, new but quite distinctive congregations in twenty-first-century England. At the outset, I was not sure whether the linking of two different ideas was achievable, but I now believe that I have produced something of value for the Anglo-Catholic part of the Church of England. I have aimed to show that church planting fits within both the historical tradition of Anglo-Catholicism, and contemporary diocesan mission initiatives, about which some Anglo-Catholics are suspicious as these seem to be dominated by the Evangelical wing of the Church. At this point, I need to stress that I am not denigrating the work of such churches; rather I want to strike a balance and show that there are other parts of the Church of England that plant churches and should be continuing to do so in increasing numbers. Some of the contemporary tensions within the Church of England around growth, the role of the parish in mission and the perceived managerialism criticized by Martyn Percy and discussed earlier, may seem to be antithetical to Anglo-Catholic ecclesiology, but I have attempted in this book to show that they can be surmounted or possibly even ignored as being irrelevant. It can be inferred that if the local church is dynamically driving a church plant, it follows that its vision should be at the forefront.

In the historical survey, I have placed Richard Temple West and Richard Foster in the wider Victorian context of the Oxford Movement and its later development; without an understanding of this context, it would be difficult to appreciate the work that both of them did to extend the mission of the Church as well as to understand the foundation on which current Anglo-Catholic worship and practice are built. West planted a new church in a very deprived area of west London which aimed to replicate some of the style of the worship of All Saints, Margaret

Street. The descriptions that I have given show that it was not without success, although there must always be a caveat around the make-up of the congregation and that applies equally today. The church of St Mary Magdalene still stands today and provides regular worship. The Victorian slums no longer exist but they have been replaced by a large estate of social housing, a large proportion of which is occupied by asylum seekers and others in need of support; some still reckon the estate to be "dangerous", so there are still some similarities in the area in which the church works.[1] So, in terms of deprivation and challenge, it is therefore almost a twenty-first-century replication of its Victorian predecessor. The building has suffered decay over the years but is currently in the process of being restored both as a beautiful place for Anglo-Catholic worship, as its architect G. E. Street intended, and also as a cultural and arts venue. Just as West made the church a centre for support in the area of social need, so today, as most of these needs have been generally subsumed into state provision, through the National Health Service, the Department of Work and Pensions or local authority social services departments, its mission is to support cultural and artistic activity in west London as well as maintaining a significant Christian presence in the area. Physically, it still dominates the landscape on the southern side of the Grand Union Canal, west of Paddington Station.

The memory of Richard Foster continues to live on as some of the churches he contributed to are still in use today; St Barnabas, Walthamstow, the church he paid for outright in 1902, is a key example. It is an active, outward-looking church, very much as Foster would have expected. It describes itself thus: "We are an inclusive church, which accepts the ministry of women priests and women bishops, with specialist ministries welcoming migrants and LGBT people."[2]

The large house, Homewood, where Foster lived when he moved to Chislehurst, no longer exists as it and its surrounding extensive lands have been redeveloped, but the two lodges at the entrance to the former drive are still occupied. During my research, I discovered that the Chislehurst Society, the local heritage and amenity society, had published an article

---

[1]   Comments by a recent vicar.

[2]   On the church website.

about Foster in its Winter 2014 newsletter, based on that house and the surviving lodges. I contacted the editor, and at her request, I contributed a fuller and more detailed account of Foster's life and activities for its Spring edition in 2020. So even in this way Foster's personal legacy lives on and continues his witness to the Christian faith.

Throughout this research I had to maintain an awareness that my main purpose in attending these churches was as a researcher with a specific brief. It would have been so easy and indeed personally rewarding to become more deeply involved in helping with their development. For a participant observer, there is always the danger of "going native".[3] This then defeats the objectivity of the exercise as the researcher then becomes a protagonist and so produces a biased result. Undertaking participant observation means that there is always a careful balance that has to be maintained between participation and observation. This balance must be kept to the fore in every engagement.

The thematic analysis of the findings in the previous chapter has identified what I consider to be transferable themes, although not in any literalist and inflexible fashion, between what impelled West and Foster to support the building of new churches and the contemporary church planting context. What is needed now is a more general application and interpretation of these themes for the wider Anglo-Catholic constituency.

Where next?

When considering Anglo-Catholic church planting and growth, there needs to be a consideration that even before 1994, Anglo-Catholics have been divided over the ordination of women to the priesthood and subsequently the consecration of women as bishops. This has caused significant damage to Anglo-Catholic witness as so much energy was being devoted to, and wasted on, these internal matters. A number of

---

[3]   "The problem of 'going native', refers to the fact that a researcher will cease to be a researcher and will become a full-time group participant." <https://wps. pearsoned.co.uk/ema_uk_he_plummer_sociology_5/205/52631/13473713. cw/content/index.html>, accessed 24 January 2023.

groups were set up to support opposing views. On the traditionalist side are "Forward in Faith" and "The Society under the patronage of Saint Wilfrid and Saint Hilda".[4] These hold together the parishes which have petitioned for "Alternative Episcopal Oversight" in the Anglo-Catholic wing of the Church of England.[5]

"Anglican Catholic Future" is the more liberal organization. It sees the divisions within Anglo-Catholicism as something to be bridged. It states its belief that the time has come for the implicit Catholic identity of the Church of England to be made explicit. "We look back to the Oxford Movement and the tradition on which it was built, and forward to the revitalization of our church and nation as we recall our secularizing culture to its spiritual inheritance."[6]

What is significant in my view is that "Forward in Faith" and "Anglican Catholic Future" worked together to organize a conference on Anglo-Catholic mission in September 2018. In her introduction to a book based on the papers and conversations at this conference, Susan Lucas states:

> The conference sought to articulate positively what is distinctive
> about a Catholic understanding of mission, in a language in

---

[4] The Society is not a membership organization. It is supported and financed by Forward in Faith and administered by its director. Those who support the aims of The Society are asked to support its work by joining Forward in Faith. It aims to promote and maintain Catholic teaching and practice within the Church of England, to provide episcopal oversight to which churches, institutions and individuals will freely submit themselves, and to guarantee a ministry in the historic apostolic succession in which they can have confidence. This oversight is provided by three Provincial Episcopal Visitors as well as the Bishop of Fulham in London. The PEVs have the role of assistant bishops in most English dioceses.

[5] There is a parallel arrangement for Conservative Evangelicals, who reject the ordination of women on the grounds that men and women have "complementary ministries" so women should not be holding leadership and teaching positions in the Church. This is now overseen by the Suffragan Bishop of Ebbsfleet (formerly Maidstone) who has an England-wide role.

[6] <https://angcathfuture.org/>, accessed 24 January 2023.

which all "tribes" of Catholics in the Church of England would feel at home, yet in an inclusive and generous way, seeking to converse with others.[7]

The book then expands on a number of themes and sees them as uniting the different emphases within Anglo-Catholicism in a shared vision for mission and growth. It is in this spirit of common mission and understanding that I want to underpin these recommendations.

It has already been commented that Anglo-Catholic church planting is quite haphazard and does not have the cohesion of the Evangelical plants, originating from Holy Trinity, Brompton and other similar churches. Most Anglo-Catholic church planters are isolated and, in many cases, feel quite vulnerable. Evidence of this can be found in Fr Francis's comments noted earlier about the lack of financial support, the response that Fr Stephen received when he questioned church growth, and Fr Sam's experience of support from his sponsoring parish. My first recommendation is that there should be *an organized network for Anglo-Catholic church planters*, where they can support each other and share their ideas about what has worked. The role of a pioneer is a hard one and if the only networks of support do not align with their ecclesiology, that makes the task even more difficult and potentially lonely. I acknowledge that there are a number of networks in existence, such as that sponsored by the Church Mission Society, but their emphases are not always in line with the way that Anglo-Catholics would see their engagement with mission and worship.[8] As evidence of the need for such a network I note that each of the three priests with whom I worked for this research felt isolated in some way as a leader of a church plant outside what is considered the mainstream of church planting.

My second recommendation is that to oversee and support such a network, *some organization needs to be established which would focus on support for church planting or other growth initiatives in an Anglo-Catholic*

---

[7] Susan Lucas (ed.), *God's Church in the World: The Gift of Catholic Mission* (Norwich: Canterbury Press, 2020), p. x.

[8] <https://pioneer.churchmissionsociety.org/pioneer-community/>, accessed 24 January 2023.

context. This could well be something which Forward in Faith and Anglican Futures could jointly coordinate with episcopal sponsorship from the traditionalist and liberal wings of Anglo-Catholicism, as well as financial support through the funding that the Church Commissioners have provided for the development of mission initiatives. There needs to be some proactive leadership in this area.

Thirdly, it is necessary *to identify as many as possible church plants from Anglo-Catholic churches in order to involve and support them.* From experience, as I was planning this research, it was a very difficult task and there was little centralized knowledge. Very much of my initial work relied on internet searches, finding contacts and then contacts of contacts. The way forward would need to have the active collaboration of Diocesan Directors of Mission or those with similar responsibilities, or via the Mission Department at Church House. This should not be a difficult task but one that needs coordination and commitment. The inclusion of Anglo-Catholic clergy in Diocesan or National Departments of Mission would undoubtedly aid this.

Fourthly, to launch such a network and support group, *a conference should be arranged to ensure maximum impact.* This is the best way to ensure wide coverage and engagement across England. It must be positively supported both by the range of Anglo-Catholic organizations and by dioceses. Again, it would be a positive move to have a number of episcopal sponsors.[9]

My final recommendation is to recognize the importance of *the sharing of good practice.* This links in some ways with the network outlined as the first recommendation but needs to be more than this. It must be evidenced and supported by actual case studies and other descriptions of the lived experience of real churches and their plants. So often in what are claimed to be new initiatives, both in the secular world but also in the world of the Church, there is little notice taken of what others have done previously in similar situations or whether such initiatives had actually

---

[9]   As a way of starting this process, I wrote to the *Church Times* in autumn 2022 to see if there was any interest in such a virtual support group. I had over 30 replies, and we meet via Zoom about every six weeks to share ideas and support.

been successful. To use an overworked and hackneyed phrase, "the wheel keeps being reinvented".

I offer these five recommendations as a way forward to ensure that Anglo-Catholic church plants receive the same level of external support as those in other parts of the Church of England. The establishment of such support must not be left to particular interest or churchmanship groups; it should be a national church priority. As I remarked in my introduction, *From Anecdote to Evidence* in 2014 said this about Anglo-Catholic church planting: "This model is still being developed and there is on-going reflection about what planting means in an Anglo-Catholic context."[10] This statement provides an external justification for this research and its conclusions. It is to be noted that nothing formally has been done in this area in the seven years since this report. As is the case with so many other reports, many of its recommendations have been ignored—in this case to the detriment of Anglo-Catholics.

In this chapter, I have sought to summarize the results that I have identified from the whole of my project and to make some practical recommendations. I believe that these recommendations are feasible and relatively easy to implement as long as there is a willingness to do so. I hope that this book will make some sort of contribution to bringing this about. This would significantly encourage Anglo-Catholic church planting in the Church of England by learning both from the historical activities of men like West and Foster and from the contemporary experiences of other church planters. Above all, church planting has to be seen, not as a mark of enthusiasm, or to be a sign of "live" church; it should be one of the many ways in which the knowledge of the gospel of the Kingdom of God can be extended in England.

---

[10] *From Anecdote to Evidence: Findings from the Church Growth Research Programme 2011–2013* (London: The Church Commissioners for England, 2014), p. 20.

Bibliography

Ammerman, Nancy et al., *Studying Congregations: A New Handbook* (Nashville, TN: Abingdon Press, 1998).

Armentrout, Donald S. and Robert Boak Slocum (eds), *An Episcopal Dictionary of the Church: A User-Friendly Reference for Episcopalians* (New York: Church Publishing, 2000).

Astley, Jeff and Leslie J. Francis, *Exploring Ordinary Theology: Everyday Christian Believing and the Church* (Farnham: Ashgate, 2013).

Bass, Dorothy C. and Craig R. Dykstra, *For Life Abundant: Practical Theology, Theological Education and Christian Ministry* (Grand Rapids, MI: William B. Eerdmans, 2008).

Bayes, Paul and Tim Sledge, *Mission-shaped Parish: Traditional Church in a Changing Context* (London: Church House Publishing, 2006).

Bevans, Stephen B. and Roger Schroeder, *Constants in Context: A Theology of Mission for Today* (Maryknoll, NY: Orbis Books, 2004).

Booth, Charles, *Life and Labour of the People in London, Third Series: Religious Influences* (London: Macmillan & Co. Ltd, 1902).

Bosch, David Jacobus, *Transforming Mission: Paradigm Shifts in Theology of Mission—Twentieth Anniversary Edition* (Maryknoll, NY: Orbis Books, 2011).

Bowen, Desmond, *The Idea of the Victorian Church: A Study of the Church of England, 1833–1889* (Montreal: McGill University Press, 1968).

Breaking New Ground: Church Planting in the Church of England (London: Church House Publishing, 1994).

Bretherton, Luke, "Coming to Judgement: Methodological Reflections on the Relationship between Ecclesiology, Ethnography and Political Theory", *Modern Theology* 28:2 (2012), pp. 167–96.

Brown, Callum G., *The Death of Christian Britain: Understanding Secularisation 1800–2000* (London: Routledge, 2001).

Brown, Stewart J., Peter Nockles and James Pereiro (eds), *The Oxford Handbook of the Oxford Movement* (Oxford: Oxford University Press, 2017).

Bruce, Steve, *Secularization: In Defence of an Unfashionable Theory* (Oxford: Oxford University Press, 2011).

Cameron, Helen et al., *Talking about God in Practice: Theological Action Research and Practical Theology* (London: SCM Press, 2010).

Carter, T. T., *Richard Temple West—A Record of Life and Work* (London: J. Masters & Co., 1895).

Chapman, Mark, Sathianathan Clarke and Martyn Percy, *The Oxford Handbook of Anglican Studies* (Oxford: Oxford University Press, 2015).

Church Growth Research Project (Oxford: The Oxford Centre for Ecclesiology and Practical Theology, 2014).

Church of England, *Statistics for Mission* <https://www.churchofengland.org/about/research-and-statistics/key-areas-research#church-attendance-statistics>, accessed 24 January 2023.

Common Worship (London: Church House Publishing, 2000).

Croft, Steven J. L. (ed.), *Mission-shaped Questions: Defining Issues for Today's Church* (London: Church House Publishing, 2008).

Croft, Steven and Ian Mobsby (eds), *Fresh Expressions in the Sacramental Tradition* (Norwich: Canterbury Press, 2009).

Davie, Grace, *The Sociology of Religion: A Critical Agenda* (London: SAGE Publications Ltd., 2013).

Davie, Grace, *Religion in Britain: A Persistent Paradox* (Chichester: John Wiley & Sons, 2015).

Davison, Andrew and Alison Milbank, *For the Parish: A Critique of Fresh Expressions* (London: SCM Press, 2010).

Dulles, Avery, *Models of the Church* (Dublin: Gill & Macmillan, 1976).

Faith in the City: A Call for Action (London: Church House Publishing, 1985).

Flett, John G., *The Witness of God* (Grand Rapids, MI: William B. Eerdmans, 2010).

Flew, Sarah, *Philanthropy and the Funding of the Church of England, 1856–1914* (London: Pickering & Chatto, 2015).

Foster, Richard, *Some Wants of the Church At Home and Abroad: With Suggestions How to Supply Them* (London: Rivingtons, 1881).

Foster, W. F., *Richard Foster* (London: Eyre & Spottiswood Ltd, 1914) (private circulation).

From Anecdote to Evidence: Findings from the Church Growth Research Programme 2011–2013 (London: The Church Commissioners for England, 2014).

Gill, Robin, *The Myth of the Empty Church* (London: SPCK, 1993).

Gittoes, Julie, Brutus Green, James Heard and Ian Mobsby, *Generous Ecclesiology: Church, World and the Kingdom of God* (London: SCM Press, 2013).

Goodhew, David (ed.), *Church Growth in Britain: 1980 to the Present* (Farnham: Ashgate, 2012).

Goodhew, David (ed.), *Towards a Theology of Church Growth* (Farnham: Ashgate, 2015).

Goodhew, David and Rob Barward-Symmons, *New Churches in the North East* (Durham: Centre for Church Growth Research, 2015).

Goodhew, David and Anthony-Paul Cooper (eds), *The Desecularisation of the City* (Abingdon: Routledge, 2019).

Guest, Mathew, Karin Tusting and Linda Woodhead, *Congregational Studies in the UK: Christianity in a Post-Christian Context* (Aldershot: Ashgate, 2004).

Healy, Nicholas J., *Church, World and the Christian Life* (Cambridge: Cambridge University Press, 2000).

Herring, George, *What was the Oxford Movement?* (London: Continuum, 2002).

Herring, George, *The Oxford Movement in Practice* (Oxford: Oxford University Press, 2016).

Hibbert, Richard Yates, "The Place of Church Planting in Mission: Towards a Theological Framework", *Evangelical Review of Theology* 33 (2009), pp. 316–31.

Hill, Monica, *How to Plant Churches* (London: MARC Europe, 1984).

Hope, Susan, *Mission-Shaped Spirituality: The Transforming Power of Mission* (London: Church House Publishing, 2006).

Hopewell, James F., *Congregation: Stories and Structures* (London: SCM Press, 1988).

Hopkins, Bob, *Church Planting 1: Models for Mission in the Church of England* (Bramcote: Grove, 1988).

Hull, John M., *Mission-Shaped Church: A Theological Response* (London: SCM Press, 2006).

Inglis, Kenneth Stanley, *Churches and the Working Class in Victorian England* (London: Routledge & Kegan Paul, 1963).

Jedrzejewski, Jan, *Thomas Hardy and the Church* (London: Palgrave Macmillan, 1996).

Kilpin, Juliet and Stuart Murray, *Church Planting in the Inner City: The Urban Expression Story* (Cambridge: Grove Books, 2007).

King, Fergus J., "Mission-Shaped or Paul-Shaped? Apostolic Challenges to the Mission-Shaped Church", *Journal of Anglican Studies* 9 (2011), pp. 223–46.

Lings, George, *Church Planting: Past, Present and Future* (Cambridge: Grove Books, 2003).

Lings, George, *Church Planting in the UK since 2000: Reviewing the First Decade* (Cambridge: Grove Books, 2012).

Lings, George, *The Day of Small Things* (Sheffield: Church Army Publishing, 2016).

Litten, Julian W. S., *St Barnabas and St James the Greater* (Walthamstow: The PCC of St Barnabas and St James the Greater, 2003).

Lloyd, Roger, *The Church of England 1900–1965* (London: SCM Press, 1966).

Lucas, Susan (ed.), *God's Church in the World: The Gift of Catholic Mission* (Norwich: Canterbury Press, 2020).

McGavran, Donald A., *Understanding Church Growth* (Grand Rapids, MI: William B. Eerdmans, 1970).

McIlhiney, David B., *A Gentleman in Every Slum* (Alison Park, PA: Pickwick Publications, 1988).

McLeod, Hugh, *Religion and Society in England, 1850–1914* (Basingstoke: Macmillan, 1996).

Marti, Gerardo, "Found Theologies versus Imposed Theologies: Remarks on Theology and Ethnography from a Sociological Perspective", *Ecclesial Practices* 3 (2016), pp. 157–72.

Mather, F., "Georgian Churchmanship Reconsidered: Some Variations in Anglican Public Worship 1714–1830", *Journal of Ecclesiastical History* 36:2 (1985), pp. 255–83.

Milbank, John, "Stale Expressions: The Management-Shaped Church", *Studies in Christian Ethics* 21 (2008), pp. 117–28.

Miller, Vincent Jude, *Consuming Religion: Christian Faith and Practice in a Consumer Culture* (New York and London: Continuum, 2003).

Mission and Public Affairs Council, *Mission-Shaped Church: Church Planting and Fresh Expressions of Church in a Changing Context* (London: Church House Publishing, 2004).

Moynagh, Michael with Philip Harrold, *Church for Every Context: An Introduction to Theology and Practice* (London: SCM Press, 2012).

Moynagh, Michael, *Being Church, Doing Life: Creating Gospel Communities where Life Happens* (Oxford: Monarch Books, 2014).

Mudie-Smith, Richard (ed.), *The Religious Life of London* (London: Hodder & Stoughton, 1904).

Nelstrop, Louise and Martyn Percy, *Evaluating Fresh Expressions: Explorations in Emerging Church* (Norwich: Canterbury Press, 2008).

Nockles, Peter B., *The Oxford Movement in Context: Anglican High Churchmanship 1760–1857* (Cambridge: Cambridge University Press, 1994).

Ollard, S. L., *A Short History of the Oxford Movement* (London: Mowbray, 1932).

Osmer, Richard Robert, *Practical Theology: An Introduction* (Grand Rapids, MI: William B. Eerdmans, 2008).

Paas, Stefan, "Church renewal by church planting: the significance of church planting for the future of Christianity in Europe", *Theology Today* 68 (2008), pp. 467–7.

Percy, Martyn, *Shaping the Church: The Promise of Implicit Theology* (Farnham: Ashgate, 2010).

Percy, Martyn, "Growth and management in the Church of England: some comments", *Modern Believing* 55 (2014), pp. 257–70.

Pickering, W. S. F., *Anglo-Catholicism: A Study in Religious Ambiguity* (London: Routledge, 1989).

Potter, P. and Ian Mobsby, *Doorways to the Sacred: Developing Sacramentality in Fresh Expressions of Church* (Norwich: Canterbury Press, 2017).

Pytches, D. and B. Skinner, *New Wineskins* (Guildford: Eagle, 1991).

Ramsey, A. M., "John Henry Newman and the Oxford Movement", *Anglican and Episcopal History* 59:3 (1990), pp. 330–44.

Reed, John Shelton, *Glorious Battle: The Cultural Politics of Victorian Anglo-Catholicism* (Nashville, TN: Nashville University Press, 1996).

Rowell, Geoffrey, *The Vision Glorious* (Oxford: The Clarendon Press, 1991).

Rumsey, Andrew, *An Anglican Theology of Place* (London: SCM Press, 2017).

Saxby, Steven, *Anglican Church Building in Victorian Walthamstow* (London: Walthamstow Historical Society, 2014).

Schuster, Jürgen, "Karl Hartenstein: Mission with a Focus on the End", *Mission Studies* 19:1 (2002), pp. 53–82.

Scotland, N. D., *Recovering the Ground* (Chorleywood: Kingdom Power Trust Publications, 1995).

Scott, William, *Fifty Years at St Mary Magdalene, Paddington* (London: H. G. Saunders & Son, 1918).

Snook, Susan Brown, "Reaching New People through Church Planting", *Anglican Theological Review* 92 (2010), pp. 111–16.

Strhan, Anna, "The metropolis and evangelical life: coherence and fragmentation in the 'lost city of London'", *Religion 4* 3:3 (2013), pp. 331–52.

Strong, Rowan (ed.), *The Oxford History of Anglicanism, Volume III: Partisan Anglicanism and its Global Expansion 1829—c.1914* (Oxford: Oxford University Press, 2017).

Swinton, John and Harriet Mowat, *Practical Theology and Qualitative Research*, 2nd edn (London: SCM Press, 2016).

Thorlby, Tim, *Love, Sweat and Tears* (London: Centre for Theology & Community, 2016).

Thorlby, Tim, *A Time to Sow* (London: Centre for Theology & Community, 2017).

Underhill, Evelyn, *Worship* (London: Nisbet & Co. Ltd, 1936).

Volf, Miroslav, *Exclusion and Embrace* (Nashville, TN: Abingdon, 1996).

Walford, Rex, *The Growth of "New London" in Suburban Middlesex (1918–1945) and the Response of the Church of England* (Lewiston, NY and Lampeter: Edwin Mellen Press, 2007).

Walker, Andrew, *Telling the Story: Gospel, Mission and Culture* (London: SPCK, 1996).

Walker, John, *Testing Fresh Expressions: Identity and Transformation* (Farnham: Ashgate, 2014).

Walsh, John, Colin Haydon and Stephen Taylor (eds), *The Church of England, c.1689–c.1833: From Toleration to Tractarianism* (Cambridge: Cambridge University Press, 1993).

Ward, Pete, *Participation and Mediation: A Practical Theology for the Liquid Church* (London: SCM Press, 2008).

Ward, Pete, *Perspectives on Ecclesiology and Ethnography* (Grand Rapids, MI: William B. Eerdmans, 2012).

Ward, Pete, *Introducing Practical Theology: Mission, Ministry, and the Life of the Church* (Grand Rapids, MI: Baker Academic, 2017).

Wolffe, John, "The Chicken or the Egg? Building Anglican Churches and Building Congregations in a Victorian London Suburb", *Material Religion* 9:1 (2013), pp. 36–59.

Woodward, James and Stephen Pattison (eds), *The Blackwell Reader in Pastoral and Practical Theology* (Oxford: Blackwell Publishing Ltd, 2000).

Wright, N. T., *Broken Signposts* (London: SPCK, 2020).

Yates, Nigel, *Anglican Ritualism in Victorian Britain, 1830–1910* (Oxford: Clarendon Press, 1999).

Printed by BoD™in Norderstedt, Germany